How to Hire and Keep Great People

YOUR GO-TO GUIDE FOR FINDING GREAT PEOPLE, DESIGNING GREAT CULTURE, AND BUILDING YOUR DREAM TEAM

Mitch Gray

Book Layout ©2021 BookDesignTemplates.com

How to Hire and Keep Great People/ Mitch Gray. —1st ed.
ISBN 978-1-6671-8683-2

Contents

This book is dedicated to two people who radically shaped and changed my view on leadership, people, and the power of the workplace:

Terry and Jackie Manz- thank you for taking a chance on a young man who thought he knew everything about leadership yet realized he had everything to learn. Your thoughts, encouragement, support, and teachings changed my life. Thank you.

I want to acknowledge my advanced reader and editing team. They were unwavering in their mission to make sure this book was clear on the message of how to hire and keep great people. Without the help of these amazing people, this book would have never evolved into what you now see. Thank you team. Job well done!

Chantelle Botha

Greg Ward

Beth Koenig (study guide development)

Chris Ippolito

Miguel Caraballo

Alisa Boswell- Gore (editor)

HOW TO HIRE AND KEEP
GREAT PEOPLE

DESIGN GREAT
CULTURE

Culture matters,
because people
matter.

FIND GREAT
PEOPLE

You can find
great people;
you just need
to learn how.

BUILD A
GREAT TEAM

Your job as
a leader is to
work yourself
out of a job.

Culture matters.

The most powerful element of an organization is the element most leaders often ignore: Culture.

Mitch Gray

The Story Behind How to Hire & Keep Great People

Hey friend-

I'm Mitch and I want to take a minute to say 'thank you' for investing your time, money, and energy into this book. There are millions of books in the world that you could be reading, but you chose this one. Words cannot express the gratitude I feel knowing you have begun the journey of becoming a better leader, learning to hire people that align with your organization, and committed to developing those people to become great.

Books are an interesting form of communication. As a writer, the goal is to choose words, craft sentences, and shape context that is intriguing, thought provoking and inspiring. That can be difficult because we aren't having a two way conversation.

I'm writing.
You're reading.

And I hope you find something on these pages that brings new thought and new opportunity to how you live, lead, and serve.

But I want to do something different. I've never read a book where the author gave some background or insight to the meaning of the book. Most books offer a paragraph or two about the author and may begin with an introduction to prepare the reader, but I think it's appropriate for you to know more about who I am, my journey, why I wrote this book, and what I hope this book does for you.

So let's give it a shot.

This is why I created 'How to Hire and Keep Great People.'

CHAPTER 1

Everything is Spiritual

I'm just a pastor at heart.

From the time I was 10 years old, all I wanted to do was be a pastor. Even at that young age, I could feel the hurt, pain, confusion and agony of others. As if there was a deep part of me that was connected with humanity in a different way than those around me.

The problem with dreams and passions and ideas is you only have the capacity of relating to them within your current perception of life. My compassion and heart for inspiring others as a young boy within my culture equated to the profession of becoming a pastor.

My childhood culture was very religious. But more than religion, our family was centered around the idea of serving others, accepting others, and loving others. We believed that by loving and serving others we were able to spread goodness in the world.

But this is a book about business. Isn't it?

Well- sort of.

In all honesty, this is a book about people. About you, as a leader. About the people who may go to work for you each day. About the people who purchase your products or services. This is really a book about the business of people.

Anytime you tell the story of people, you quickly learn that people are much more than business or numbers or tasks.

Humans, by nature, are spiritual beings. I'm not talking about religion here. I'm talking about those deep, hard, contentious, emotional moments in life that take your breath away or make your blood boil or bring a tear to your eye.

The moments we all stop and consider the depth of place and time.

That is the spirituality of people.

But what does me being a pastor and spirituality and magical moments have to do with business?

That is a really great question.

You often hear leaders do their best to separate life, business, politics, and spirituality. The problem is none of them are separate. They are all elements of living and taking an active part in life. It is impossible to separate any of them, because each of them impacts the other.

Work life greatly impacts personal life. If your people are stressed at work, they take that home each night. There is no way of protecting people from the things that impact them at work.

If their personal lives are stressful, this greatly impacts work life. The stress doesn't simply leave their minds and emotions once they clock in and begin their workday. Great leaders understand that it is impossible to compartmentalize elements of life, so they create opportunities for their people to grow in every area.

The idea of creating an opportunity for growth is a spiritual idea. This concept has a depth and breadth that goes far beyond thought or emotion or stress or physicality. Growth takes place within a person long before it becomes an action or manifestation that can be seen or heard. This is the very meaning of spirituality: The exploration of the inner self.

When you begin to view spirituality as this inner dialogue and learning, you can see how spirituality greatly impacts the workplace. If you have a team filled with individuals growing spiritually, you will then have a team that becomes very successful and fulfilled with their work. They will soon become extremely high performers because of this fulfillment within.

The barrier keeping many leaders from introducing spiritual growth into their organizations is the idea of religion. Religion has nothing to do with spirituality. One can be growing spiritually and have no regard or relationship to religion. Conversely, one can also be very religious but empty and void of any spirituality. So, there is no reason to fear engaging the spiritual element of the workplace.

It is well-known that spiritually healthy people are happier people. They are also hard-working people. They bring a passion and perspective to the table of life that spiritually unhealthy people can't comprehend. Spiritually healthy employees are the greatest asset and partners an organization can have. They are positive, solution-seeking, and unifying people. They approach success and barriers much differently than those who may not be growing spiritually.

In times of chaos, you know spirituality matters. In times of need, you know spirituality matters. Yet, many often forget the role spirituality plays in creating success. Even more so, spirituality plays a powerful role in sustaining success.

Peace, perseverance, patience, teamwork, humility, and discipline are all very important factors in creating success. And each of these is a spiritual element. None are physical. None of these elements can simply be thought into existence. They must all be learned, patterned, and practiced. This is spirituality.

The practice of patience is spiritual.
The practice of discipline is spiritual.
The practice of peace is spiritual.
The practice of teamwork is spiritual.
The practice of humility is spiritual.

Spirituality already exists within your organization. You may not have recognized or accepted it, but it is present. No matter the words you use to describe it, spirituality is taking place and living within the fiber of every word spoken and action taken.

If you are struggling with finding great people, you have a spiritual problem.

If you are struggling with growing past a certain plateau, you have a spiritual problem.

If you are struggling with keeping great people, you have a spiritual problem.

If you are struggling with customer service, you have a spiritual problem.

If you are struggling with creativity, you have a spiritual problem.

All of these are spiritual problems, because they can all be solved with spiritual solutions. Culture, hiring, bettering customer service, increasing knowledge, opening the door to more creativity are all barriers that can be overcome through spiritual growth.

Finding great people is difficult for many because they lack clarity regarding their alignment and description of who they need. Clarity means you know exactly who you need, why you need them, and what they will accomplish within your business in order to find success.

Clarity and alignment are only found when you have explored the deeper parts of yourself and your business. Knowing why you exist (purpose), what you are trying to accomplish (mission), and how you will accomplish it (strategy), are all matters of spirituality.

To continue growing you must do the work within to create new strategies outside of yourself. You need a community of like-minded people ready to accomplish great things and help you achieve what you have set out to do. This is spiritual work. It is emotional work.

Have you ever experienced a moment of poor customer service? We all have. It's frustrating. We often leave the situation angry, or resentful, or vowing to never do business with that company again.

Conversely, have you ever experienced a moment of great customer service? A moment the person handled your situation with compassion and understanding? A moment where they eased your concerns and you left feeling empowered as a customer? When people are living from a place of happiness, they are much better at their work. They are far less likely to become angry with customers or co-workers. Happier, fulfilled people are much better for your business.

This is what spirituality in the workplace looks like.

It looks like compassionate customer service.
It looks like employees who are perfectly aligned with their work.
It looks like teammates celebrating each other's birthdays and life events.
It looks like sorrow when someone is hurting and joy when someone succeeds.

While many leaders ignore the idea of spirituality in the workplace, the future is showing us that the next generation of great leaders are understanding the value spirituality brings not only to their organization but more importantly, to their people.

And people are the lifeblood of any business.

Spirituality is impacting your business.
Spirituality is impacting your people.
Spirituality matters.

I tried my hand at ministry and the industry of religion. I was great at some parts. I was terrible at others. More importantly, I was miserable. During my years of trying to decide what to do with my life I fell in love with business. Even more- I fell in love with the idea of empowering leaders to empower others. Teaching them to create worlds and atmospheres in the marketplace that served others well.

This is my spiritual work. To teach you how to go to bed each night feeling like you've done something great in the world and teach you how to teach others the same.

You may not be a religious person. You may not have ever considered your business or work as spiritual. But I invite you to entertain the thought that each action you take, word you speak, and strategy you plan might impact others in a way you've never thought possible.

And considering that thought, my friend, is spiritual work.

Spirituality Matters

1- How do you value spirituality within your organization?

2- What is your perception of spirituality and the role it plays within your organizational culture?

3- What perspective do your team members have regarding spirituality in the workplace?

4- What are the advantages of recognizing the role spirituality plays in your organization?

5- How would you like to grow in this area as a leader?

CHAPTER 2

We Can't Find Good People

A few years ago I was invited to speak at a local event attended by business owners and leaders from our community.

This was the type of event where you're asked to speak but given only 15 minutes or so of time and everyone is eating and talking and socializing. Having previously attended this event, I knew what I was up against. I also knew I wanted to give each person there the most valuable 15 minutes of time possible.

I stood up, introduced myself and posed a question:

'How many of you struggle to find employees for your business.'

I had their attention. I had immediately addressed a pain point each person sitting in that room dealt with. The next 15 minutes became a Q&A session about how to find great people, how to develop them, and how to lead well.

An older gentleman in the room shared a story about how he likes to hire a few part-time high school students for his small business each year. These students normally do office work, cleaning and small tasks each day. He mentioned how it seemed over the past few years it has been difficult to find dependable teens to work.

I asked him to define dependability for us. His response was interesting:

'All they do is ask questions when you tell them what to do!' He exclaimed. So I asked him to share what types of questions these young people ask. He said 'they always want to know why I'm giving this task and how it's going to help.'

I hear this often when visiting with leaders. Leader gives a task- employee asks why this task is important- leader misconstrues this question as rebellious or undermining- employee simply wants to know that what they are doing matters.

I responded to the gentleman at this event by compassionately explaining to him that the younger generation is wonderful because they want to know that what they are being asked to do is valuable. They want to expend their energy on what is important. They want to feel like their work has purpose.

After painting this picture for him, he sat back in his chair and quietly stated, 'I guess I've never thought about that before.'

I then posed the question again, 'how many of you struggle to find good people to work for your business? Or are you simply missing the people that are right in front of you?'

"We just can't find good people!"

I've heard it a million times. From business owners, managers, and leaders in companies of all sizes.

I often ask them, "what is the greatest challenge you face?" Their response is almost always the same - We can't find good people.

I remember what it was like to wake up each morning knowing I needed to make changes to my team. I remember the feeling of excitement when I knew I had hired someone who was going to succeed at the job. You could feel it. It's a palpable energy that exists when you know you have hired someone as perfect a match as possible.

But finding these people is a learned skill. It doesn't just happen overnight. Recruiting, hiring, and developing are not talents we are born with. Learning where to find these "good people," crafting a conversation that makes them become intrigued with your organization, then having the courage to offer them a position takes practice, time, and focus.

The great thing? You can learn how to find these great people. The even better thing? You are in control of who is part of your team. Even better than these two? You not only get to choose who is on your team, but you are also in absolute control of their development and success.

This is why when business leaders tell me they can't find good people, I tell them that is a lie. They can find good people. They can find great people! Walking this earth right now are millions of great people, who would take your company to a level you've never dreamed of - if only they had the chance.

Believing you can't find good people is like saying you can't grow your business - and no successful business leader would ever make that statement.

You can find good people; you just need to learn how. There is a process and skill to seeking out employees who will change your business for the good and increase your bottom line. There is an art to finding the ones who will care about your business, lead your business, and become the type of employees you can trust to run your company. But it's up to you.

At the end of the day, you are the only person responsible for finding these great people. You may have an HR team or manager who you've put in charge of hiring, but ultimately, it is you who is responsible for who becomes part of your team.

If you've found yourself frustrated with hiring, firing, developing, and keeping people ...

If you've found yourself complaining about anyone on your team ...

If you've heard your leaders giving excuses as to why business isn't growing or employees aren't dependable or only a few are carrying the load ...

This book was written for you.

Now it's time to learn how to hire and keep great people!

Great people are everywhere

1- When was the last time you felt like you couldn't find good people?

2- What led to this perspective?

3- What actions have you taken to find good people?

4- On a scale of 1-10, how would you rate your ability to recruit great people?

5- What would you like to change about your recruiting/hiring strategies?

CHAPTER 3

Standing Desks & Bouncing Balls (Why culture matters)

There is this idea that the greatest benefits of working for a company can be listed or proven.

Insurance

Paid Time Off

Sick Leave

401K

Discounts

Swag

When most companies recruit, they quickly jump to the list of selling features that come along with working for their company. They do their best to sell people on the tangibles.

But regardless of what people may express in a job interview, the reality is people do NOT work for the tangibles. People take jobs for the tangibles - higher pay, better benefits, larger market - but they do not stay for them. So this list of selling features (aka benefits) you have spent so much time selling people is, at best, short-sighted.

So why do people stay?

People stay because of culture.

- A TINYpulse employee engagement survey revealed that employee happiness is 23.3% more correlated to connections with coworkers than direct supervisors

- BUT employees want strong management transparency, according to another TINYpulse study, where they found this transparency leads to 30% better employee retention

- Another recent study shows that 46% of HR leaders say employee burnout is responsible for up to 50% of their annual turnover

- According to Bonusly's Employee Engagement and Modern Workplace Report, highly engaged employees are 40% less likely to be looking for a job compared to actively disengaged employees

- A Gallup poll showed that 44% of employees would consider taking a job with a different company for a raise of 20% or LESS

- And a study by Willis Towers Watson tells us that more than 70% of high-retention-risk employees say they will have to leave their current organization to advance their career

This data is telling us a story. A human story. A story that the truth is simple: No matter what benefits or pay you offer someone, they will not stay if your culture doesn't value them. Period.

Year after year, study after study, we are seeing this story unfold. Yet still, companies miss the truth of this story even today. It's time you make sure your company isn't falling for the myth that benefits and money keep people around.

Culture has the single greatest impact on every single element and person that makes your company function. Culture has the single greatest impact on your bottom line. Culture matters, because people matter. At the end of the day, we are all in the same business, regardless of profession.

We are all in the people business.

We are engaging and interacting and communing and fellowshipping and bartering and conversing and creating this crazy thing we call life. Each person brings their own experience and perspective, and each of us shares our own story of how we have arrived at this moment in time. People matter.

Because people matter, business matters. The way you do business matters.

Years ago, businesses began to toss around this idea about "culture." Companies hired health consultants to create meal plans and gyms and yoga classes that offered support to employees. They replaced office chairs with round bouncy balls and brought in desks that could be raised so their people could stand when they were working. Weekly meetings began to include walking programs and incentives to motivate better health. Everyone was wearing step counters, and soda machines were removed. While each of these actions and programs are great, they aren't culture. They can be elements of a healthy culture but they, in and of themselves, do not bring with them a culture of success, health, and positivity.

Culture is really about success and oppression and permission and empowerment and movement and energy. Culture is palpable. You can cut it with a knife. Culture is about positivity and negativity. Hope or hopelessness. Happiness or depression. You have either a negative, oppressive culture or a positive, empowering culture. There is no in-between. Culture is beautiful, because it cannot remain stagnant. It is always moving toward either negativity or positivity, and you can sense this movement without any doubt.

This is why the gravest mistake companies make is ignoring culture.

Before you spend time on product development, growth plans, business strategy, or marketing, you must spend time defining your culture. Without a strong, positive culture, every plan you create will fail. It may take time. You may have enough resources to tread water for a while. But history has told us time and again that without positive culture, you will fail.

This is the old saying at its best: "If you don't believe in something, you'll fall for anything." If you don't have a strong, positive culture to guide each of your plans, each of your hires, and every moment of education and engagement, you will eventually fail.

Failure isn't just about closing down a business or filing for bankruptcy. Failure manifests itself through a myriad of platforms.

Stress

Lack of sleep

Unhealthy habits

Anger

Turnover of employees

Inconsistent productivity

Burnout

Customer complaints

Bad product

Negativity

Untimely delivery

Damaged goods ....

I could go on.

So many have too broad a definition regarding failure. Failure to some is the idea of losing everything or giving up. While taking pride in the idea of beating the competition or not giving up as markers of success, they are under-valuing the small failures upon which they have built their organization. They blame high turnover rates on not being able to find good people. They blame low sales on not being able to find qualified salespeople. They blame slow productivity on distribution or shipping. They blame bad product on someone else. Yet, in their mind, they aren't failing simply because they open the doors each morning.

Failure isn't found in the end solution of moving on.

 Failure is found in the lack of day to day ability to identify a problem, take responsibility, and create a solution.

This is why culture matters.

A strong, positive culture holds us accountable for taking responsibility and finding solutions.

Healthy culture leaves no room for pointing the finger in any direction except at one's self. Healthy culture allows your team to hold you, as a leader, accountable, as well as holding each other accountable. A healthy culture is about eradicating all signs of negativity and creating an environment that nurtures growth and hope. A healthy culture is about failing only because we continually take risks and live from high idealism. Our risks are accounted for, because our culture allows for growth and movement ahead.

The most powerful element of an organization is the element most leaders often ignore: Culture.

DEFINE YOUR CULTURE

How have you defined your culture?

How have you clarified and shared your message of culture?

Do you have high turnover?

How have you defined your culture?

You should be able to answer this clearly in a few sentences or less within 10 seconds of me asking. It should be clearcut. Everyone on your team should know this. If there is any hesitation at all, that is your answer.

How have you clarified your message of culture?

Does your team know, without any doubt, what your culture is? Is it a one-liner that everyone has memorized? Do your customers know what you stand for? Without any doubt? Is the response from your team and customer base larger than the product you sell? If not, you have not clarified your message. No one understands what you stand for or why you exist.

What is your historical turnover rate?

This is often the most simple way to measure culture. The data shows clearly that companies with a positive, healthy culture carry that reputation in the marketplace, and their employees remain loyal and excited about their work. This is very clear when we measure companies with a healthy culture. The public flocks to their company to engage as either a customer or an employee. Turnover for these companies is very low, if not rare. Why? People love to work where they are appreciated and empowered. If you have high turnover, I can guarantee you have a culture issue.

Take some time to measure your culture. Visit with your team and ask them how they feel working with you, representing your company. Listening to your people and taking action on their feedback is positive regardless of your current culture. If you're sensing negativity, then listening and responding is the first step you should take. If you're sensing positivity, then this will only help in guiding your company to heights unknown. Culture matters, and it will dictate the path your company will travel for decades to come.

The most valuable element of an organization

1- When you began your organization, or the position you hold currently, how much time did you spend designing your culture?

2- What does 'measurable success' look like for each team member on a daily basis?

3- What is your plan of action for teaching the idea of measurable success to your team?

4- How do you set each day up for measurable success with each team member?

5- Describe your culture. What sticks out to you about what you have described? What would you rethink or reframe? What would you keep?

CHAPTER 4

The Real Reason People Work

Year after year, study after study, the people tell you their story - you just aren't listening.

More than 50% of organizations globally have difficulty retaining their employees (Willis Towers Watson).

49% of HR and hiring managers have identified needing better training programs as their number one need for attention within the company (Onepoll).

73% of companies revamp their onboarding to improve employee retention (East Tenth Group).

One-third of new hires quit their job after about six months (BambooHR).

4 out of 5 business leaders rank employee retention as important or urgent.

Read these data statements again. Start doing the math or working through the process of simplistic deduction.

Here is what you will soon discover: None of this is making sense!

The cost to replace a highly trained employee can cost upwards of 200% of their annual salary! Read that again - 200%!

Rather than using resources to invest in someone who can do a job well, you end up spending resources on recruiting, hiring, training, on-boarding, enrolling in more benefits packages, and developing new people when hiring the right people from the beginning and investing in their success would end the cycle of turnover madness!

This is the reason company leaders rank employee retention as important or urgent. At the same time, employees continue leaving as if they are walking through a conveyor belt of opportunity.

Here's the truth - they aren't. Opportunity isn't knocking on everyone's door. People are not leaving, because the money tree has come their way. They are leaving because of something greater, something much less measurable than money. And this is exactly where what should be simplistic deduction becomes a mess.

I am going to teach you how to keep employees longer in a way they will be much more satisfied and your company will grow because of it.

Before any of that, let's begin here, because the next sentence you read will matter more than any other sentence in this book:

You are struggling to keep employees, because you don't understand why people work.

There is a why behind everything in life. A motivation. An understanding that pushes you to move and act and live. This why - no matter what area of life we are discussing - is the single greatest motivating factor. If someone doesn't understand the why, they soon burn out or get bored or move on. Understanding the why is everything.

As a leader, understanding this why might be even more critical. Knowing the why behind your people allows you to plan more strategically, empower them more directionally, and motivate them to greater results. When an employee notices that you have taken the time to understand their why, they will do all they can to participate and play their part in building your company beyond your imagination.

Everything is about the why. Everything.

So why do people work? This is the question you must answer to make sense of all the data we began with. This is the question you must answer to begin alleviating the challenges you are facing with your team. You can almost dissolve the frustration of employee retention if you know the why.

People work for many reasons. Your team is not unlike you. The motivation for work is not predicated on education or experience. The motivation for work is based on human behavior. And we all have these same human behaviors, regardless of economic status or career position. Humans are humans. We all behave the same. The description of those behaviors may change. The manifestation of those behaviors may be different. But the behaviors are simply part of our DNA. We are human, and we all work for the same reason.

So why do people work?

Money? Yes

Purpose? Yes.

Community? Yes.

Identity? Yes.

Independence? Yes.

But these are the simple answers. These are the shallow, run-of-the-mill responses you will hear from most. These are the responses you get to the "why" when no one wants to truly consider what is at play.

If the five reasons above were truly what everything is about, then why do people leave jobs after six months? That isn't enough time to truly know how any of those five reasons are going to play out. Money is the easiest of answers. After all, we have bills to pay, and the last time I asked the electric company to take goodwill and a promise for my bill, they politely declined. Money is the currency for economic stabili-ty.

But money isn't the deeper why.

Let's talk about the real reasons people work. The reasons that most leaders are not considering. The reasons leaders, for the most part, have not built as the foundation for their business.

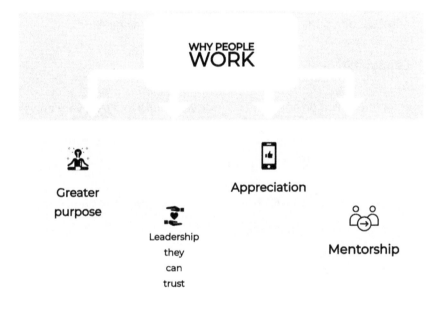

WHY PEOPLE WORK

Greater purpose

Appreciation

Leadership they can trust

Mentorship

Greater purpose

People take a job for money. They stay because of purpose. The very people you need the most are often the ones walking out the door faster than you can hire. This shows a lack of purpose. If people are leaving your company within six months of being hired, one of two things is happening: You don't know how to hire, or you lack clarity of mission and purpose. Usually, it's both.

We all want to build something greater than ourselves. We want to be a part of a community that succeeds and accomplishes something great in the world. Your team wants a vision to believe in, and evermore, they want to be an intricate part of building that vision. They want to go home at night knowing they did something great. This is the purpose, and purpose outweighs money every single time.

Leadership they can trust

A recent Gallup poll of over one million workers told us a very powerful story: 75% of people who left their job voluntarily did so because of managers and leaders, not the job.

Think about that - and let's be real - your people are leaving because of you or your leadership team.

People want leadership they can trust. They want to know they aren't wasting their time doing mundane tasks that won't be recognized. Your janitor wants to know that his work is valued. Your assistant wants to know that her work is appreciated. Your sales team wants to know that their performance is based on more than just numbers and commissions. Your board of directors wants to know they are supporting a larger vision.

Leadership matters more than you may ever know.

People will follow a passionate, clear, authentic, compassionate leader to the ends of the earth. Don't think this only applies to war generals and football coaches. This principle applies to every type of leadership you can name. People will take part in something they believe in but only if leadership allows.

Appreciation

Let's make this easy - two of the single most powerful words you can offer your team are these -

Thank you.

Positive reinforcement is the most powerful action you can take. Showing your team appreciation with a sincere "thank you" will be the greatest investment you can make. If you need to motivate someone, show them more appreciation. If you need to correct someone, use appreciation to build trust so when correction is needed, they know you have their best interest at heart. If you need to support someone, show them appreciation.

Appreciation is never the wrong thing to do. I have heard leaders express concerns about becoming too soft or developing a reputation for being too nice if they show appreciation. This attitude is more a reflection of your own insecurity than it is a reality of how people will respond. I have never witnessed a negative response from showing appreciation. Ever.

Appreciation will increase production, morale, longevity, happiness, and profits. Appreciation is the long game. This is why so few play it. But you're here for the long game, right? Let appreciation guide the way.

Mentorship

LinkedIn's Workforce Learning Reports states that 93% of employees would stay at a company longer if it invested in their careers. 93%!!!!! That's incredible!

Let's reflect on our first motivation for the "why" behind working - Greater Purpose.

People want an opportunity. They want to know that what they are expending energy on each day will bring about something greater. As a leader, you are in the perfect position to influence those who work with you. Your opinions, perspective, and feedback matter greatly! Your people want to better themselves, gain knowledge, become more effective at their work, and more impactful in the world. When you set your team up for success, they will reward you with greater effort.

Companies are missing opportunities for mentorship each day. You see this when you read the job descriptions and requirements listed on job sites. Most companies have become lazy in how they hire and are searching for shortcuts in adding to their teams. This leads to the data we began this chapter with. So what is the remedy? How can companies ensure their efforts are no longer empty or duplicated just a few months after hiring someone?

They can invest in their people.

Many of the jobs listed on job boards do NOT need the certifications and qualifications listed. People are smart. People learn quickly. Take away all of these certifications and qualifications and simply hire people based on character, energy, and creativity. When you hire someone based on these qualities, then invest in them; mentor them so they can receive the certifications and qualifications needed.

You will not only have great people; you will have great people who you have now invested in. People you have mentored and grown in your company. People who will feel valued when they show up each day. These are the people you want. These are the people who will grow your company.

Everything is about the why

1- Before reading this book, what was your perception about why people work?

2- How is 'How to Hire and Keep Great People' reshaping your perspective of why people work?

3- What action can you take to give your team members a feeling of greater purpose each day?

4- What are three steps you and your leadership can take to show appreciation each day?

5- Does your organization have a mentorship program? If not, why? How could you design a program to ensure each team member is mentored?

Designing Your Culture with Intention

Your people know one thing for sure- culture matters.

The mistake many companies of all sizes make is creating a culture about them and not their people. Owners, CEOs, human resources, managers, and board members begin creating this environment they think will be successful. They create systems and training's and tasks and job descriptions, rarely thinking to include the very people that will be using those systems and training's or doing those tasks and jobs.

Why would you create an environment that impacts so many while never asking the ones being impacted how they would like to function within this very environment?

It's lazy, at best.

It's selfish, at worst.

More importantly, it's a recipe for disaster.

You can grow a company that makes millions and millions of dollars within a terrible culture. Many business leaders have. You can develop a structure and culture that cares little about people and much about the bottom line and be "successful." If this is your path of choice, this book is NOT for you. This book is about people. Period. People are the lifeblood of your business. Employees. Customers. Clients. Shareholders. Without people, you have nothing.

The greatest product in the world is simply a dust collector without people.

And culture is the barometer for how much you value those people.

So how do you create, design, and implement a culture that cares? How do you develop and build a culture that empowers people? This is what business is really about. Empowerment. Regardless of your guiding principle in business - profit, growth, charity, ministry, change - you are empowering someone. You are giving responsibility to someone. You're already influencing those very people who are building your dreams.

This influence isn't in question. What is in question is HOW you are influencing people. What is in question is your legacy as a leader. Because legacy is what truly matters. Your story. Their story. Culture.

So, how do you design a culture that empowers your team? How do you set up an ecosystem where people thrive rather than simply exist?

How do you ensure your investment in recruiting, hiring, and developing brings a return? Ideally, these are the questions business leaders would ask when planning a new business. Unfortunately, reality shows us that culture is NOT on the minds of business leaders when planning their new endeavor. Yet, months into this new business, they quickly begin seeing the red flags of bad culture, whether they realize it or not.

Low sales performance

Employees late to work

High turnover

Frustrated managers

Negative customer experience

The list goes on and on.

These are all red flags of bad culture. They are all a direct reflection of leadership, both management and ownership. The greatest lesson you can learn as an owner is simple: YOU are directly responsible for every single thing that takes place within your company. For some business leaders, this is a great burden. If you own a corporation filled with multiple stores or sites, thousands of employees, and hundreds of departments, this is an incredible burden to carry. But it is your burden. Every action and experience is a direct reflection of your leadership. Period.

For those who are managers, this is the lesson you must accept: YOU are directly responsible and accountable for those within your circle of influence. Every hire, every sale, every experience, every mistake - they are all a reflection of your leadership, and you must carry that responsibility with honor and compassion. You are the one who answers to ownership, not your people. You may be running a team of three or a team of 300. Regardless, it is your calling as a leader to make sure each person on your team has everything they need to be successful.

Why are these lessons important? What do they have to do with culture?

What I've noticed in working with hundreds of leaders from a variety of leadership backgrounds and in working with thousands of employees, is that culture begins and ends with leadership.

If there is confusion in the workplace,

if there is clarity in the workplace,

if there is a misunderstanding in the workplace,

if there is total connectivity in the workplace,

it is all a direct reflection of leadership.

Show me a team that is unified and functions with clarity and does their part to the fullest extent, and I will show you leadership who does the same - leadership who goes above and beyond to carry the responsibility of their people. I may not ever meet these leaders or owners, but I know, by the reflection of their team, they are strong leaders who people are passionate to work for.

This is culture. This is the foundation of a successful business. They have low turnover and highly successful people. When team members leave this type of company, they are leaving for very FEW reasons. One of them is not because of a bad experience. This is a small glimpse of what a healthy culture looks like: Empowering your people to step into success, regardless if that success is with your company or not.

Years ago, when I was managing for a high fashion retail company, I hired a young man who was a high school student at the time. He was an incredibly successful young man, high achieving in both sports and the classroom, and he took part in many extracurricular activities and was beloved by all of his teachers. I remember calling his references to find out more about him, and call after call was the same story over and over. Seemingly, every single adult in this young man's life would willingly pay money to have him work for them. Teachers loved him. Coaches loved him. Family and friends loved him. He was hardworking, dependable, and personable, one of those kids you spend a lifetime searching for.

I hired him. We quickly developed a connection and built a relationship that became much more mentor/mentee rather than employer/employee. I soon found myself scheduling my shift with him as much as possible, so I could pour into him as much as possible. And let's be honest, as leaders, we love nothing more than being around positive people who positively impact our business.

Sundays were a slim day on the schedule for our store, so I would often open the store with this young man. I went to church on Sunday morning. He had either family or sports stuff on Sunday mornings. So, after I was done with church, I would hurry to pick up some tacos for our lunch and rush to the store. We would open the store, stuff down some tacos, and get ready to crush the day. It was always a great time working with this young man, and we sold a ton of clothes together.

A few years went by, and he graduated high school then moved into his new career. Following in his father's footsteps, he joined the United States Air Force, and over the next 10 years, he found great success, quickly moving up the ranks and experiencing the world while enjoying his beautiful family and life. At the writing of this book, he is a senior master sergeant in the USAF. It has been beautiful to watch his life unfold.

During his last promotion, I sent him a message, congratulating him on this next phase and his hard work. His response was incredibly humbling. He mentioned how I had inspired him and taught him much about leadership and how to impact people. He mentioned that he often uses what he learned from me in his work with those under his leadership.

Think about this for a second - I had absolutely nothing to do with this young man's success. I had zero to do with his accomplishments in the Air Force. Yet, he took the time to recognize the lessons he learned as a 16, 17, 18-year-old kid and that he still uses those lessons to this day. THIS is what legacy is all about. As an owner, manager, CEO, you will make an impact. It will be an impact of negativity or positivity. The question becomes, how do you want to impact the people you lead?

This small example of influence shows the value of strong, positive culture in the workplace. If I was a jerk or rampaging manager or a turn and burn employer or didn't bring this young man lunch Sunday after Sunday, do you think he would remember the lessons he learned some 20 years later? No. He might remember me, but it would not be in a positive light.

Leader - you have to know your why, for yourself and your business. This why leads you to designing your culture. Your culture is made up of many elements, but the ones that should become foundational are what matters.

ELEMENTS
OF CULTURE

How
you treat
others

How you
engage with
others

How
you speak
to others

How you
lead others

Spend some time reflecting on these areas of your life. Searching within is where the hard work takes place. But it's the work that truly matters and can change the direction of your company for the better. When you reflect on the impact you are having on the lives of others, when you measure how you have positioned yourself and your team, you become much more aware of how to build sustainable success for your organization. Not only financial success, but success that attracts great people and great customers.

I've shown you that culture is valuable.

I've shown you why culture matters.

I've shown you the legacy that great culture can leave.

Now let's design your culture.

We are making this as easy as possible. Work through these steps. Write things down. Write them down again. Create and recreate until you know, beyond any doubt, this is how you want your environment to exist.

The culture barometer

1- Why is culture so valuable in the workplace?

2- How could a healthy culture impact your business?

3- Reflect on the foundational elements of culture mentioned in this section. How can your response to these elements change the way you lead?

4- How would you define your leadership style?

5- How does your leadership style relate to creating a positive culture?

6- Is there anything that might be a disconnect in developing a culture of empowerment and positivity?

Culture Design 101

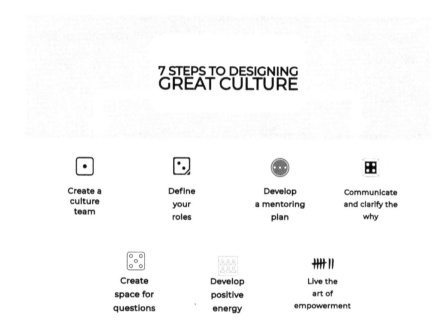

7 STEPS TO DESIGNING GREAT CULTURE

Create a culture team

Define your roles

Develop a mentoring plan

Communicate and clarify the why

Create space for questions

Develop positive energy

Live the art of empowerment

This is your culture design playbook. Keep it simple, yet build depth. Designing culture is not complicated when you have clarity on a few things:

- The experience you want to create for your team each day

- The experience you want to create for your customers/clients each moment

- The experience you, as a leader, want to create and experience each day

When you have clarity on the type of experience you want each person who comes in contact with your team or product to have, you then fill in the blanks as to how these experiences will come to life.

That is culture.

But you can't be the only voice and mind creating this culture. You need the input, ideas, experiences and perspective of others. When you begin designing culture, you must first gather a team that can add to the picture you are painting of the experiences people will have.

Step 1- Create a Culture Team

The first step you should always take when designing culture is to gather more voices to the table. At minimum, you will involve your leadership team. A best practice is including employees outside of your leadership team as well.

This is the list you should begin with:

Everyone on your leadership team
One person from each department

One person from each level

Even or proportionate split of male, female, transgender representation

Even or proportionate split of ethnicities represented

Even split in age demographic

Designing your culture is possibly the most valuable step in creating a successful business. Positive culture sets your organization up for sustainability. Positive culture creates an environment that will last. For this reason, you want voices from each demographic of your team. You need a wide array of perspectives. You need a wide selection of experiences. Your team of janitors may recognize things your leadership team may never experience. Your part-time, high school employee may bring a thought to the table your upper management person would never consider. Your summer intern might have a perspective no one else sees.

When designing culture, more voices bring more value.

Value matters.

Let's breakdown your Culture Team and why each element is important. You must recognize the value in each of these voices. Two points are being made here:

> If you cannot represent each of these demographics, it may be time for you to measure the makeup of your team and company. You want wide representation as much as possible.

> You are giving voice to every single area of your organization/business. If this brings about fear within, remember that fear is a direct reflection of your internal belief system. It's making you uncomfortable. But if you want to take your business to the next level, you must learn to live with the things that make you uncomfortable.

- **All leadership team**

  This is a no brainer. I have experienced so many business owners who keep their leadership team in the dark. Don't let this be you. Vulnerability and inclusion are huge strengths to great leadership. You need the voice of your leaders. If you feel you can't trust them, then you either have the wrong people in those positions, or you have some internal work to do within yourself.

- **One person from each department**

  Regardless of the size of your business/organization, you have people leading various elements or departments within your company. Those leaders need to be involved in designing your culture. They are your eyes and ears regarding day-to-day operations. They are making decisions that reflect you and your business.

- **One person from each level**

  Larger businesses may consist of multiple levels. Upper management (C-suite), middle management, department heads, salaried employees, hourly employees, full-time, part-time, seasonal, project-based, interns. These employees represent levels within your company. They all have different experiences, perspectives, and expertise. You need these voices at the table when designing culture. Why? Because these are the people building your dream.

Your company represents a skyscraper building. As the owner, everyone sees you in the highest suite in the building. You may pride yourself on being relational and connected, but the employees at the lower end of the building see you as the top suite face. No matter what you hope people see, this is reality. This example paints a picture of each level of your company. No matter how large or small. This is why you need every level represented in designing your culture. You cannot possibly understand everything each person in your company experiences. As you invite them to take part in the conversation, the chasm will narrow and the relationships will grow. This is how you create a positive culture.

- **Even split of gender, ethnicity, age**
  This is an element of measurement. Who have you built your company around? Is your leadership team mostly men? Are most of your lower-level employees of a certain ethnicity? Have you paved the way to create opportunities for women of color? Are you leading the charge in supporting transgender brothers and sisters?

Many business leaders don't consider these elements. After all, we don't hire "based on ethnicity, religion, political affiliation or gender," right? The reality is, the history shows, most organizations do. You may be the one who has participated in the hard work and created a new way of living, but for the most part, organizations are far behind in where we should be at this point in humanity.

So this element of your Culture Team is a challenge. How diverse can you make this conversation of culture? The more diverse, the more effective. If you bring your people to the table to discuss culture and around the table are mostly white men, a few women, and no people of color, you have a problem. Don't fear the challenge! Take it as an opportunity to usher in a new way of thinking and conversation. You will never go wrong with diversity. Ever.

Step 2- Define your roles

Every single role within your company should be so well defined that any employee can be asked and clearly give a response to what those roles are. No one should ever respond with "I'm not sure what they do" or "I think this is the department you want."

You have been on this call, I'm sure. The call where you dial 1-800 whatever to contact customer service about an issue regarding that awesome new thing you ordered online. You wait for 30 minutes then get transferred to a million different people, and two hours later, you still have no answers. Yes, that call.

When your team lacks defined roles, this is the exact experience they, and your customers, go through. No one knows the answers; no one knows who has the answer, or no one wants to take responsibility for making a decision. This type of culture will increase employee turnover and decrease customer experience. No one is happy. Define your roles. No matter the size of your organization.

Defining roles within your Culture Team is a great place to begin learning how to distinguish responsibilities, actions and accountability. What areas will your Culture Team be leading? Who will be responsible for specific actions? How will everyone take part in holding each other accountable? How can your Culture Team lead the way in creating an environment of empowerment, responsibility, inclusion, and diversity?

Taking the time to define roles within your culture and leadership teams will set the playbook for defining roles within your organization.

Step 3- Develop a mentoring plan

Mentoring is the gateway to longevity.

93% of employees would stay at a company longer if it invested in their careers. You could take this one single step from this book and drastically change your organization. Organizations who have set up mentoring programs, offered educational opportunities, or invested financially in the growth of their people, lower employee turnover and raise employee satisfaction in often immeasurable numbers. It's difficult to measure the pride and joy of someone when they receive their college education. It is impossible to measure the gratitude of people within your organization who know they have an opportunity to grow with you.

Creating an in-house mentoring program is simple, sustainable, and cheap. You are already paying people to make leadership-type decisions, lead programs, interact with customers, so take your best people and set up a program that mentors others. Your program can be that simple or as complex as offering scholarships or continuing education. You get to choose. However you decide to create your mentoring program, the message here is to create one.

Step 4- Communicate and clarify the why

Some call this their mission. Others call it their vision. And yet others choose to make this their purpose. Call it what you will - at the end of the day - this is your why for existing - your purpose. It could be related to your product or the pain point that brought your product into creation. It could be a more humanistic idea of how you are bettering society. You must know your why.

Even more, every single person who interacts with your company should know your why. Employees, customers, clients, partners, contractors. They should all know why you exist. Marketing 101 teaches us the most impactful form of marketing is word-of-mouth. This will never change. It may take form in a variety of ways, but word-of-mouth is marketing money. When others know your why, you have now given even more power to word-of-mouth marketing.

Employees should know your why by heart. Customers should hear and see this why every time they experience your company. Don't be shy about it. Put it on signs, commercials, social media, but more importantly, put it into action. Let your why breathe life into your culture. It will change everything about the experience people have with your company.

Step 5- Create space for questions

The power of growth lies within asking questions.

The greatest path to empowering your team is inviting them to ask questions. Questions measure the willingness of people as well as open the door to learning. Questions should not be an expectation. Rather, they should be modeled, then, invited.

You often have to teach others how to ask questions. Question-asking is an art form. Too many leaders make the mistake of expecting people to ask questions, yet they have not taken the time to teach people how to ask questions. The art of question-asking must be a part of the fabric of your culture. Teach your employees what questions to ask, how to ask them, and who to ask. Once permitted to ask questions, most employees will learn to ask their questions based on their curiosity and growth. This is a sign of a healthy culture.

Learn an action - mimic an action - take responsibility for action - action leads to growth

When you not only give power to questions but teach people how to ask them, you will radically change how your team communicates and how each person grows.

Step 6- Develop Positive Energy

You can cut energy with a knife.

You have been there. You walk into a place, feel something not quite right, turn around and leave.

You have also been here. You walk by a place of business, feel the draw of energy, and find your curiosity leading you through the door.

It happens to all of us. We all have a story of both good and bad energy. From the lunch room as kids to shopping to conversations with strangers. We can feel energy at all levels of our being. Which makes sense, because everything is made of energy.

If energy matters so much, then why don't people invest more time in creating an energy that draws rather than repels? You have the power and choice to create your energy. You have the responsibility of empowering others to create the energy you want within your company. This is a choice.

I love teaching teams about energy. About how to create good energy. Energy that draws. My favorite example of energy is restaurants. Two restaurants are side-by-side. One parking lot is filled with cars and a line out the door, and the place next door has flickering lights and no cars parked. Which restaurant are you going to choose?

It's simple, right?

THIS is energy.

It's as if, within our human DNA, lies this curiosity that knows, beyond all doubt, how to detect energy. Again, you have experienced this very phenomenon. So, it's time to use this power for the good of your company. Create energy that attracts your team, attracts customers, and attracts business.

Step 7- Live the art of empowerment

We began the steps of designing your culture by bringing people to the table. Another reason inclusion and diversity are so valuable to your Culture Team is it gives hope to others. This is called empowerment. I have experienced too many leaders who fear empowering others. I cannot count how many leaders have told me, in various forms, they fear empowering their people, because someone may be better than them and take their job. I have even heard owners of companies make this statement!

It happens more often than it should, leaders leading from a position of fear rather than empowerment.

I was fortunate as a young professional to work around, for, and with leaders who taught me a very important element of great leadership:

Your job as a leader is to work yourself out of a job.

The underlying message of this lesson was simple: Your #1 priority as a leader is to empower your people. When people feel empowered, they feel motivated. When they feel motivated, they become inspired. When they become inspired, they perform at incredibly high levels.

And guess what? I've never met a leader who empowered their people so greatly they lost a job. Ever.

This is your roadmap to designing a culture that people will love to work within, and customers are eager to engage.

Within this culture, hiring will become less of a challenge, because people won't leave, and when they do, there will be a waiting list of people who are ready to work.

Within this culture, customers and clients will seek a great experience and shout it from the mountaintops when they do.

Within this culture, people will perform at levels unseen, because they are motivated, empowered, hopeful, and have taken ownership of making this vision come to life.

Within this culture, revenue and profit can't help but grow, because everyone invested will do everything within their power to make sure they take care of those who gave them an opportunity - You.

It's time to design your culture. You will not succeed at anything else until this is done. Culture provides inspiration, accountability, boundaries, and measurement for progress. Without an intentionally designed culture, you have no foundation for success.

Developing your culture team

1- Do you currently have a culture team? If not, begin making a list of who you would include on this team and why.

2- Who is your possible culture team made of? What does it look like? Have you represented the diversity described in this section?

3- What role does each person on your team play? Do they understand their role clearly?

4- How have you clarified and communicated your organization's why (mantra, mission/vision statement)? What steps could you take to better communicate and clarify?

5- How will your team actively create positive energy? What programs or plans of action could you implement to create this energy?

CHAPTER 6

More Than Fancy Buildings, Pretty Flowers & Bright Lights (The art of leadership and interpersonal growth)

About 20 years ago, the talk of culture began gaining momentum in the corporate world. Companies were hiring self-help coaches to keep their teams positive, physical trainers to develop workout programs, and nutritionists to help employees design the most optimum diets for the workday.

Bouncing balls replaced office chairs; fluorescent lighting was benched for skylights, and plastic trees in the hallways were thrown away for actual living plants. This new idea and direction seemingly worked for a while, but not long after the material changes, many began too notice something was still missing.

What happened 15-20 years ago regarding company culture is similar to what happens to many who seek plastic surgery for their physical body: If you don't heal the root of the problem, no amount of surface change matters.

There is a reason doctors send plastic surgery patients to a therapist before any procedure takes place. They need to know the patient is prepared, not only for the long journey of healing but also prepared internally for what led them to this moment in time. There is usually a reason emotionally, mentally, and spiritually that leads people to desire change to their physical body. Doctors need to make sure the patient is prepared for the journey ahead.

What happened to corporations 20 years ago is that many gave their company culture plastic surgery. Unfortunately, they didn't see the therapist beforehand. Rather than taking part in the difficult work of changing from the inside, they bought balls and flowers and changed out soda for water, thinking these surface changes were the solution to the problem of culture.

The challenge that so many overlook when it comes to culture is culture is a human problem, not a stuff problem.

Culture is directly related to humanity. We can all reflect on our families or the community that impacted us as children and immediately identify our culture. That culture may be positive or negative or in between, but regardless, we can identify our culture. That culture, whatever it was, shaped us. It impacted us to our very core. This is human behavior.

Bouncing balls and flowers and skylights might make for a much more effective work environment, but at the end of the day, these things are simply to be used as results of a culture change, NOT the reason for the culture change. Culture change is found in behavioral change, which is why so many companies miss the whole idea of designing a strong company culture.

Business leaders are often very good at just that - business. They often forget that the lifeblood of every business is people, and people carry with them human behavior. So to truly be great at business, you must first be great at being human. Sure, there are business minds in the history of humanity who created what many thought was a successful business empire and were also bad at dealing with people. When you dig deep into the stories of these business minds, you find how terribly they treated their employees, how poorly they engaged their customers, and how the only thing they were successful at was robbing from people to build their mountains of money. So in reality, many of these "great" business minds really aren't successful at all. They don't understand humanity.

And humanity is what culture is all about.

Strong, vibrant, positive company culture values their people so greatly that no one feels like just a number. People working for companies who value human behavior feel empowered, destined, and like they have a place in this world.

Companies who care more about fancy buildings, pretty flowers, and bright lights than the people who are building their business have missed the point completely when it comes to company culture. But years ago, those were the things leaders thought made company culture. Sadly, many companies still hold to this belief, and it shows in their numbers and performance.

Learning to develop culture with depth takes reflection. The problem with reflection is it calls for us to take inventory of our personal beliefs, personal motivations, and reasons for doing what we find ourselves doing. Doing interpersonal work is not fun. It is difficult. Walking through what has led us to this moment in time often leads to issues we do not want to deal with.

What does interpersonal work have to do with leadership? With business? With hiring or employees or revenue?

The simple answer: Everything.

You may not realize, or even care to realize, that your internal systems of existing greatly impact everything you do - from decisions you make to people you impact to things you create. All of us are guided by our internal systems, consciously or unconsciously. For this reason, finding a way to measure and grow personally matters when it comes to leadership. But this isn't the work most of us want to do. It is especially not the work we feel is related to our impact and success. We like to compartmentalize most things in life, because we believe that, with compartmentalization, comes the ability to ignore the issues at hand.

Interpersonal health is the elephant in the room many in leadership positions do not want to address. While most leaders will say it is valuable, connecting interpersonal health to business is a game few like to play. But if we are talking about how to design healthy culture, how to create a place where people love to show up each day, how to position your business for sustainable, long-term growth, then inter-personal work is where the road begins. You cannot ignore it.

The reason so many companies bought into culture simply existing of lights and flowers and water machines and training programs is they forgot to start at the beginning of true growth. True growth only takes place when each individual is willing to explore self and step into the work needed to become a healthy, fully alive individual.

The problem with individual growth, from a leadership perspective, is the idea of individualism. And many leaders do not understand how to navigate individualism. It's much easier to simply tell people what to do, how to do it, and when to do it. For many, this is the definition of clarity - demands and deadlines and discipline.

But demands, deadlines, and discipline are not clarity. They are the result of clarity.

After working on self and growing to a level of healthy leadership abili-ty - the ability to empower others - clarity then gives way to individual-ism, because individualism is desperately needed for long term growth. For it is only through individualism that you find idealism, in-novation, and creativity. Individualism is essential for building commu-nity. Each person needs to know that what they take part in each day brings value to their community, to their team. The only way to deliver value to another is to provide the space needed for them to be who they are, not who you want them to be.

Empowering individualism within each person on your team will lead to each person taking great pride in their work and purpose. Pride and purpose are a sure path to great success.

Business is art. Business is creative. And you need every single per-son partnering with you in your business to bring their greatest ability to work every single day. This is only possible through individualism.

But this type of leadership and culture begins with you, the leader. It begins with leaders having the courage to step into the work of self, to find a humility they may have never found before and walk the path of leading change and growth internally. Then, and only then, are leaders able to extend the idea of growth to others. Anything outside of this type of leadership is shallow. It has no sustainable power, and growth is empty. If you want staying power as a leader, begin the work of in-terpersonal growth.

I once sat in a leadership team meeting with a small business owner, and I heard a statement I have heard a hundred times before. As the conversation was flowing and strategy was being planned, someone in the meeting shared a thought. One of the owners of the business responded a bit aggressively, rejecting the idea this manager offered. Another owner looked at the manager and said, "Oh, don't worry! It's just business. It's not personal."

We have all heard the "it's just business; it's not personal" statement in one form or another. Maybe from a boss, or other leaders, or on a show or podcast. But here's the truth to this statement: It might be business, but it is always personal.

The following statement is the single greatest piece of advice I can give you as a leader. Highlight it. Underline it. Write it on paper and hang it on your mirror. If you will remember this one sentence, it will change everything about how you lead, no matter the size of your business. Corporate or corner store, this one sentence will change your life when leading others.

Everything is connected. Nothing is separate.

As an owner, you may have the ability to compartmentalize your life. You have other aspects to deal with during the day. You may be juggling so many different areas of your life that walking into a 30-minute meeting and sharing your thoughts quickly is simply a check of the box for the day. Because of this, you may say it's not personal; it's just business.

But there are people at the table who are taking it personally. And there is nothing wrong with that. Your employees spend more time with your company, building your dreams, achieving the goals you have set than they do with their own families. They are possibly choosing to exchange their own dreams for building your dreams, because bills need to be paid and mouths need to be fed. So it IS personal. Every minute of every day is personal. It's personal, because each person under your leadership has chosen to build your empire, no matter how big or small. They are giving their lives to you when they could easily choose another path.

No matter how well you may pay your people, no matter how strong your culture, the moment you lose sight of how personal business really is, you have lost the game. Your team and leaders can smell that mistake miles away. Business is personal, because energy is being invested. People are expending their energy each day to build business for you. And the return on the investment of energy isn't measured in money or vacation days or benefits.

The return on energy invested is measured in value and appreciation.

When you make the statement or show through action that business isn't personal, what you are telling your people is they don't matter. Their ideas don't matter. Their stress doesn't matter. When they stay up late at night thinking of ways to do their job better, that doesn't matter. When they miss a family event for work, that doesn't matter.

Telling people this 'isn't personal; it's only business' is telling them they don't matter.

EVERYTHING is connected. NOTHING is separate. And your people take that VERY seriously.

When you do the interpersonal work of learning, living with humility, and committing to growth, you are well on your way to being the type of leader people dream of working with.

When you take the time to reflect on yourself and how you want to truly impact the world, you will begin the process of becoming a leader that measurably impacts others for the better.

This is much more than fancy buildings, pretty flowers, and bright lights. This is about much more than increasing revenue and productivity. This is about changing lives, paying bills, feeding mouths, and provision.

As an employer, you have decided to impact lives in a way you may not even conceive. You are providing an opportunity for parents to provide for their children, for dreamers to fulfill lifelong dreams, for college graduates to step into the world of opportunity, for future entrepreneurs to learn how to do business positively.

As a leader, you are shaping the world we live in regardless of your motivation. You are making an impact. This is why culture is so incredibly important. This is why every decision you make is so valuable.

Leadership is a burden. Too many in leadership positions have lost sight of this: Leadership is a responsibility that changes lives.

Everything is connected.

Everything matters.

And it begins with the culture you choose to design.

Humanity is what culture is all about

1- What opportunities could your organization provide for your team that would create opportunities for interpersonal growth?

2- What steps are you taking daily to provide greater depths of clarity? The greater knowledge and understanding a team has, the less they have to stop and think. The less they have to stop and think, the more often they simply respond to situations based on the clarity they have.

3- How can you use the idea of 'business is art' to positively impact your organization?

4- Does your organization operate from a perspective of separation or connection? How could everyone become more connected?

CHAPTER 7

Professor for a Day (Learning to find where good people exist)

"Mr. Gray," she asked, "what is your favorite thing about being a manager?"

I found myself standing in front of a classroom of about 25 eager college students ready to hear what I had to say about fashion. But not just fashion. They wanted to know what it was like to lead a team, to make schedules, to work budgets, and grow a business.

They wanted to know everything.

I, myself, was a 22-year-old, eager-to-learn leader. Having moved up quickly within the company I worked for at the time, I was running a multi-million dollar high fashion retail store and learning to use my leadership skills in the best way I could. Things moved quickly in that business. I had pivoted from a kid who simply wanted to be a preacher to now running a store with little experience and understanding of what everything meant.

But I knew people. I knew how to lead. And really, that's all that mattered.

I had taken over a store that was extremely underperforming in every area. It was located in a small town market, housed in a small shopping mall with few shopping options. But this company believed in this store. They believed that something great could be built at this store, and I had been tasked to be the builder.

I had never hired anyone.
I had never fired anyone.
I had never really trained anyone.
I had never recruited anyone to work for me.

After taking over this store, I soon found myself struggling to find really good people. My approach quickly became to hire as many people as possible and see who had staying power. I turned and burned hundreds of employees in my first few years. It was the only way I knew to exist in the situation.

Then I stumbled onto something about how to hire people:

 You have to find where good people exist and meet them there.

This changed everything when it came to recruiting. I got lucky with a few of my hires in my first year, and quickly noticed how they would invite their friends to shop with them. These friends loved fashion and would stop by whenever they were able. I then began to ask questions. I began to investigate the commonalities these new customers had with the employees I had hired. They all loved fashion. They were friendly. And they seemed to be the kind of people I would want representing my shop.

But there was one final commonality: They were all college students. This was the circle of friends that my team members lived with, hung out with, went to school with, experienced life with. Not long before this discovery, I had read in a business book about seeking people who live life with your best employees. It's the old saying: "Birds of a feather flock together." When talking about recruiting with my district manager at the time, he would recite this saying to me constantly. He knew I needed to have that message drilled into me, so I could understand what was taking place.

Soon after this discovery, I asked one of my assistants why she thought college students make such good teammates. It was a revelation to me at the time. She listed things like career interest, the opportunity to apply their education to real-world circumstances; they just need money, and even something as small as "they are bored." This was powerful to me. I could finally put skin on the idea of job fairs and interview meetings and canvassing campuses - all of the stuff big businesses did in the world- or so I thought.

But now, I could be the one finding these opportunities.

I then asked my employees who were college students to connect me with any of their professors who taught a class that, in any way, was tied to what I did as a manager. Business classes, textile classes, management classes, marketing classes, economic classes - I didn't care; I just needed an audience that would listen to what I had to offer, and who wanted experience, management possibility, future opportunity, a great work environment, and a ton of fun.

I soon found myself in front of a classroom of college students ready to learn and a professor who was excited to have someone from the community speaking. It was a win/win. In that first class, we began with textiles and why they are important in fashion. We discussed how they could apply what they are learning to a variety of career paths. I wanted to open their mind to the idea that they are not stuck in one path in life. The world is full of opportunities, and yes, even a textiles class can teach you so much about the world around you.

Then, in the middle of a conversation about textiles and fashion sense and design, came the question.

"Mr. Gray," she asked, "what is your favorite thing about being a manager?"

"That's simple," I responded. "It's people."

That was my first experience at becoming a professor for a day. Over the next four years, I spoke at over 50 classes and events at area colleges and universities and in local communities. Those opportunities became a treasure trove for recruiting both employees and shoppers. I can't remember a single event that didn't return some sort of reward.

While these moments are wonderful memories and were powerful experiences, those memories and experiences weren't the greatest takeaways from those events. Yes, I would get excited when we recruited someone to shop or work with us, but those were simply affirmations of my development as a leader.

The greatest lesson I learned during those years was simple:

People are the lifeblood of any organization.

During those years, I built relationships that I have kept for well over 20 years, some of them close relationships. I learned that no matter how much I knew about leading or managing or selling or building a business, if I lost sight of the value of people, I would lose everything. People are the real reason we exist.

And in business, this existence of people matters more than anything else.

I believe, without any doubt, my passion for people is why I have achieved the things I have achieved in life. I believe my passion for people is the reason for every single opportunity I have been given, from leading businesses to writing books to speaking to coaching to impacting anyone I have had the honor of impacting. I firmly believe it is my passion for people that has created those opportunities in life.

But why does passion for people matter? What does a passion for people have to do with hiring and recruiting and running a business?

Countless people in the world have built great companies. They have made more money than most of us will ever see and have built empires of buildings and gathered an incredible amount of possessions. While we look at these accomplishments and could view them as measurements of success, we often forget to ask the people around them how they view the success of these empire builders.

It's easy to write a book on how to become a millionaire. It's easy to create a curriculum and course on how to upscale your business. Making money is often the easiest part. The difficult part is deciding how you are going to make your money and what people will say after you do. This matters when it comes to hiring and building a team, because what people think of you does matter!
Here's how I know:

- A Udemy study shows that nearly half of employees state they have quit a job because of bad management

- TINYpulse has shown that 40% of employees who don't rate their supervisors performance highly interview for a new job compared to just 10% who rate their supervisors performance highly

- A Gallup poll found that only two out of five employees strongly agree that their managers have made efforts to clearly define the teams role and responsibilities

The message employees give time after time is incredibly clear: It matters what they think of leadership within a company. Even more, it matters how leadership impacts their lives.

Employees are telling you blatantly they care how you live, how you treat others, and how you engage them. This is why being passionate about people matters significantly when it comes to building a team. People have an innate desire to work with someone who cares.

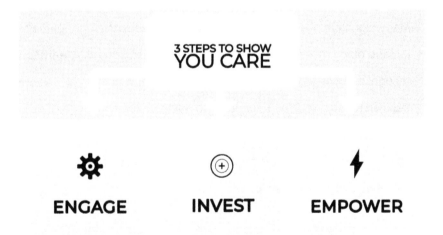

3 STEPS TO SHOW YOU CARE

ENGAGE   **INVEST**   **EMPOWER**

They measure care in three ways:

1- How you engage with them
2- How you invest in them
3- How you empower them

When an employee goes home at night, they want to feel like they've done something important in the world they exist in. They want to be exhausted from the joy of doing something that matters. Employees have a desire to work in an environment that they never want to leave.

And as a leader, you want to find yourself kicking your employees out at the end of the day.

Many signs are showing you what your employees think about their job and place of work. To become a great leader, you must learn to recognize these signs and respond to them in a way that shows your passion for people. You must learn to navigate the challenge of designing a culture that permits your employees to fully exist within that culture. Any partial existence leads to burnout, loss of interest, and inevitably, loss of an employee.

Until you understand the value of passion for people, you will constantly struggle with hiring and recruiting. You will find yourself fighting a never-ending battle of hiring the wrong people, not properly developing the right people, and losing people consistently. This is one area that has the single greatest impact on your bottom line. So, it's time to rethink how you hire.

It's time to become a professor for a day.

It's time to learn how to proactively hire people that make sense for your company.

And when they ask what your favorite part about leading is, you can then answer, "it's simply people."

Because people are the lifeblood of any business.

You have to find where good people exist

1- Do you view recruiting as a daily/lifestyle activity or only valuable when you need someone?

2- Have you designed a recruiting plan? If not, what has kept you from strategic recruiting?

3- List 5 recruiting opportunities that exist in your community?

4- Who could you contact to leverage these opportunities?

5- If the idea of recruiting is new, what steps will you take to begin recruiting great people?

6- If you currently actively recruit, what are 3 new strategies you could implement?

CHAPTER 8

Where to Find Great People (If she offers dessert)

When my kids were little, it became a running theme to see how quickly dad was going to begin asking the waitress, waiter, or salesperson questions anytime we were out to eat or shopping. Even at a young age, they figured out my game.

Once I learned the art of finding great people, my recruiting antenna was up every time I engaged someone. Finding amazing people became a challenge I took personally. I enjoyed the idea of hand-selecting my all-star team to help build the business. Once I understood how important these relationships were, I placed great value in my effort to find the best people I could.

There is a downside to this style of recruiting: You can easily lose sight of the real value of relationships and engagement with others. Yes, you are building business. You want the best people you can find working with you. But this isn't the purpose of relationships. The purpose of relationships is for the betterment of humankind. Keep this at the forefront of your mind when recruiting or teaching your team how to recruit.

I remember creating a game with myself when eating at restaurants. The game was simple: If they offer dessert, I'm going to ask how they are enjoying their job. Again, it was that simple. I can't recall how many recruiting opportunities this simple game led to. It had to have been hundreds.

Did I hire everyone I visited with? Not even close. I hired a very small percentage. The goal isn't to hire everyone you talk with. The goal is to improve your ability to find great people and to expand the opportunity for finding those great people.

Over the years of sharing recruiting ideas with business leaders, I have heard a few complaints about this approach. Let's review these complaints and discuss them, so you can gain an understanding of why actively recruiting your future team matters more than you think.

Complaint 1: I own/work for/lead a large company. We have over 2,000 employees. It is impossible to recruit for a company this size.

Response:
You have over 2,000 employees who take up hundreds of thousands of dollars a year in your budget to hire, to develop, and to give salary and benefits, yet you want to leave the control of who fills those positions to a third party or app-based product?

The larger the company, the more control you want in making sure every position matters and makes sense. The only way to do this is to train your team on how to recruit, who to recruit, and why it matters. No matter the size of your company, your team should know exactly the type of employee you're seeking. Every person on your team should be eager and willing to refer people to work for you.

Here's a simple formula to use: The larger the company, the larger the percentage of personally recruited employees you should hire.

As the owner, manager, CEO, you should be constantly recruiting people.

Every employee should be recruiting people.

Every single person working for your company, shopping with your company, or partnering with your company should be recruiting people for you on a non-stop basis. There should be a never-ending flood of referrals coming your way. And few of them should be through third party partners or app-based products. Those are simply a bonus.

Complaint 2: I'm too busy. I simply don't have time to be recruiting people.

Response:

Do you go grocery shopping? Do you eat at restaurants? Do you shop for clothes or cars or hobbies? Do you take your family shopping? Do you attend any social events? Do you attend a religious function regularly? Do you volunteer in your community? Do you talk to anyone other than yourself?

If the answer to any of these is yes, then you have time to recruit.

It's this simple: "Hey, George, I enjoyed volunteering with you today. I am always looking for great people to add to my team, so if you or anyone you know is looking for a new opportunity, please let me know!"

Again - it is this simple.

Anytime you meet someone who grabs your attention, tell them you're always looking to add great people. They may not be looking, but they know hundreds of other people. If you've engaged with them in a sincere, honest, and empathetic way, they will be eager to send people your way, because you made a positive impact on them.

People want to be part of something positive. Something much larger than their personal life. When you make a positive impact on the life of another, you have given them a story they want to share. And that matters.

Complaint 3: It costs too much for my company to recruit personally.

Response:

You're spending more money than you realize on hiring someone else to recruit and hire for you.

You know your culture. You designed it.

Your team knows your culture. They live and breathe it.

You know who you want working with you.

Your team knows who they want to work with.

> *A third party, no matter how great you communicate who and what you're looking for, cannot comprehend the make-up of your team and culture the way you or your team members can. Why? Because a third party has never experienced your culture.*

Let's measure the tangibles.

How much turnover are you facing currently?

How many of those employees who left were hired by a third party?

Look at your highest level performers, how many were hired by a third party, and how many were recruited either personally or from within?

It costs up to 200% of a high performer's salary to replace them. 200 percent! Every time you replace a high-level employee, you are wasting money.

It costs too much to replace employees. The best solution for this problem is to control who you recruit, interview, and hire.

The best system for controlling the makeup of your team is actively recruiting yourself, teaching your leaders how to recruit, and challenging your employees to recruit. This system is the single greatest way to proactively decrease employee turnover and raise performance.

No matter the size of your company, you can easily control who is being recruited and hired. It simply takes implementing a system and culture of recruiting, and it is much easier than most think.

It will save you money.

It will give you more opportunity to hand-select your team.

It will improve revenue, because you will now be hiring people who you know want to build your business.

Let's dig a little deeper on where to find great people, especially if you have not been functioning from a culture of recruiting.

Here are five places to begin looking for great people today. Each of these is an opportunity that can be tapped right away.

5 PLACES TO FIND GREAT PEOPLE

Colleges and Universities

Social media

Lifestyle recruiting

Networking groups

Within your team

Colleges and Universities

Colleges and universities are terribly underrated when it comes to recruiting and building business. Many companies make the mistake of waiting for job fairs or other career-related events to come around.

I'm challenging you to be more proactive.

The majority of college professors love hosting guest speakers. They find value in allowing their students to engage with a member of the community who is doing the work. Students love having the opportunity to ask questions, hear stories, and learn from someone who is in the real world. They are eager to put their knowledge into practice. This offers an invaluable opportunity for companies to engage and open the door for recruiting new employees.

Here's how you make it happen:

Step 1- Find any classes, areas of study, or degree programs that relate to your company.

Be open-minded about this. For instance, a business management class relates to any type of business. A finance class relates to any type of business. A human development class relates to human behavior, which relates to any type of business. A psychology class would be perfect for a manager or business owner to speak to, because you are always dealing with human issues/behavior.

Never cut yourself short on opportunity.

Step 2- Contact the head of the department or professor of a specific class.

Here is your script:

"Professor Johnson, I am Glenn Jamison- manager for Shield Glass Unlimited. I am seeking opportunities to give back to my community and would love to do so by speaking to college students. I believe your class would be a great opportunity to share my work and offer your students time to ask questions about building business, networking, and being an entrepreneur.

It would be great to visit with you about speaking to your class as a guest speaker. I look forward to hearing from you soon!"

It's that simple. This is something that can be done by anyone in your company. Regardless if you're the owner, manager, CEO, or even one of the higher-performing employees, you can step into a classroom (in person or virtually) and immediately have an audience ready to engage with you. This time is immeasurable regarding recruiting.

Step 3- Enjoy interacting with eager minds.

You've set the date. You've prepared your talk. Now it's time to enjoy the opportunity to build relationships and interact with people who are eager to learn, value your insight, and are ready to ask questions.

Make it fun. If you aren't used to giving talks, ask a friend who may have experience in this area. Talks should be engaging and offer two-way communication with your audience. If you want to go next level in this area of recruiting, feel free to send us an email and we can discuss setting up a training to prepare you to recruit at your best: mitch@mitchgraymedia.com

Networking Groups

The world is literally at your fingertips. Networking has changed drastically over the past 10 years and for the most part, the new way has opened the door to unlimited possibility. In other words, there is absolutely no reason your company should not be finding, recruiting, and hiring absolute all-stars that fit your culture perfectly.

Social media has given you an open door to hundreds of networking opportunities. Whether it be small group virtual calls, local chamber of commerce meetings, or signing up for programs to improve your leadership skills, there are countless ways to join networking groups.

Here is a great tip for you to implement within the DNA of your culture:

Each manager and leader must attend at least two networking opportunities each month. Make it a part of your culture. Be creative. Hold everyone accountable and proactively make sure you are finding the right people for your team.

Social Media

While social media can become a place of distraction and random, directionless acts, it can also be a gold mine of opportunity.

You are going to use it for recruiting in a simple way. Find and follow hashtags of topics that relate to job seeking and job finding. The magic to recruiting is going to where the people are, and the people are living on social media. They are posting about job experiences, job needs, job opportunities, companies they love shopping with, companies they've had negative experiences with, and how they wish the world worked. You want to be involved in all of these conversations. You never know where that next diamond in the rough might be, so you want to explore every area possible. Social media hashtags are filled with people seeking new opportunities.

Within your team

I've stated it before, but this time, let's shift the perspective.

You want your people recruiting, especially your highest performers. Your employees should love working at your business so much they can't help but share their experience with others. This is recruiting. But let's organize this effort, so it becomes measurable, attainable, and accountable.

Your next step is to pointedly ask your employees if they know anyone who would be a fit for the company or who might be seeking a new opportunity. It's amazing to me how few companies take this step. It's a simple question. Begin by asking your highest performing team members and respond from there.

Everyone knows someone. Everyone knows someone who would make a career change in the right situation. If you have designed a culture that empowers your people, then I promise every single one of your employees knows someone who would like that same opportunity. You will be amazed by how much impact a simple question can have on your company.

Lifestyle recruiting

This is the most simple way to find and recruit great people. And it might be the most overlooked. You spend too many hours investing in your business to NOT be constantly seeking great people to add to your team. You owe it to yourself, your employees, your owner, and your customers to continuously develop who is helping you build this dream.

The best way to do this is to always be alert. Always be watching for the person who engages you, the person who asks questions, the person who is a great storyteller, the person who suggests dessert, the person who is working incredibly hard. You and I could walk into any place of business within 10 minutes of your location and find great people. In some places, we might find 20 great people within a half hour.

This isn't some fairytale story of hopes and wishes. This is you, as a leader, learning to engage people at a different level and having the courage to open a conversation about how much they enjoy their work and if they have ever entertained another opportunity.

This is about designing a culture that is so strong and healthy, your team can't stay quiet about their experience.

This is about your customers raving about the service they received or how your product changed their lives.

This is about you positioning yourself as a leader who cares more than just about performance. You care about people, because people are the lifeblood of any business.

This is about shifting how you think when it comes to gathering your team - the team that is going to invest hard hours, money, time, energy, and life into your business. They deserve your best. And your best can only be found within.

Learn to recruit.

Teach your people to recruit.

Learn to identify and recognize the opportunities taking place all around you.

Because you never know where your next great leader might be hiding.

She might be about to ask if you're ready for dessert.

Measuring the intangibles

1- What complaints have you found yourself using when struggling to find great people?

2- What is keeping you from recruiting?

3- Have you budgeted time in your schedule for recruiting? If not, why?

4- How many hours per week are you willing to invest in finding great people?

5- How would upgrading your team change your organization or impact your business?

CHAPTER 9

Defining Who to Hire (Understanding the art of hiring)

There is an art to hiring.

There is an art to designing your culture.

There is an art to developing people.

Business is art. It is full of creative moments, intriguing design, and decisions. Possibly the greatest mistake many have made in business is they have lost sight of the art of business. Algorithms, programs, apps, and agencies have led to a lack of creativity and independence when it comes to designing business and hiring people.

But this life is about humanity. It is about spirit and emotion and thought and awareness. Algorithms, budgets, and programming will never replace the flesh and blood element of humanity. They will also never replace the flesh and blood element of business.

Because at its core - business is art.

Understanding and remembering the creative personality of business is critical when you are hiring. Hiring is about alignment, personality, culture, heart, and work ethic. The only way to understand these traits within a person and how they align with your culture is to know them. To explore them. To understand them.

To find great people, you must know how to use the tools that exist. Valuing certain tools over others at the wrong time will only cause frustration and waste time, energy, and money. Every tool is valuable, but only if you understand when and how to use them.

Third party apps can be of great use if they are used as only one element of recruiting and hiring.

Agencies can be invaluable, only if they are used in addition to in-house and lifestyle recruiting.

Everything you need to find great people is at your disposal. The mistake most people make is knowing when and how to use each of these tools.

But before you can use any tool available, you must know who you need to hire and why. Taking action before knowing the "who" or "why" is wasting energy and resources.

When you begin describing who you need to hire, most begin with a job description. This is a massive mistake. When you begin painting the picture of "who" by starting with a description of the job, you leave out the most important element of hiring - the human element. Creating a job description before describing the person you want filling that description is like writing a story with no character traits. You must know exactly who you want filling that role before defining the role.

Personality matters. Humanity matters. Far too often, the humanity concerning the position is left behind. What good is a position if you constantly hire the wrong person to do the job? The obvious answer is it isn't any good. Aligning the position with the person and the person with the position is where the magic of productivity takes place. Many of your headaches and struggles can be solved by simply understanding alignment.

Let's explore the top three mistakes people make when hiring.

THE TOP 3 MISTAKES MADE WHEN HIRING

Lack clarity on the position you are filling

Lack clarity on who you need

Underestimate the art of interviewing

Lack clarity on the position they are filling

People focus too much on a job description and not the actual day-to-day work of a position. They are worried so much about credentials and requirements and having a warm body filling a role, they lose focus on what truly matters: Aligning the right person in the right position. This alignment will remedy the majority of frustrations when it comes to hiring.

When you base your hiring on personality, work ethic, energy (presence), dependability, and aptitude for learning, it changes your approach in describing who you want to fill a role. Sure, there are a few positions that require certain certifications, degrees, and knowledge, but these roles are few and far between. The majority of jobs in the modern world do not require anything other than a dependable person showing up and willing to learn skills that will increase productivity and results.

Too many companies negate so much opportunity, because their front side expectations are far too high regarding certifications, degrees, and experience and far too low regarding character, personality, dependability, open-mindedness, and aptitude. You can teach skills. You can buy certifications. You can teach an open-minded employee how to do something. You cannot teach personality, work ethic, or attitude.

Companies who have clarity about the job they need to be done and the type of person they need to be successful have a much greater chance at success. They understand that measuring the human interest of a new hire is much more valuable than skills or education. When you have clarity about what needs to be done and who needs to do it, you open the door to an opportunity that was never before possible.

Lack clarity on who they need

Far too many leaders hire based on luck.

They have never put the effort into describing the type of employee they desire to work with. This lack of clarity in the "who" causes major negative disruption in the "how." Workflow, culture, and productivity are stopped because of misalignment. Wrong people filling the wrong positions will deliver to the doorstep of frustration very quickly.

> *You must be clear on who you want partnering with you in building success. Your focus must be on intangibles rather than tangibles. Your goal is to learn the art of hiring based on the presence of a person rather than the skills of a person.*
>
> *Remember, a skill can be taught. Attitude and aptitude cannot.*

Taking the time to describe the type of people you want to hire will eradicate much of your frustration before a hire is even made. This positions you much further ahead of the curve in hiring great people and developing them, so they have a reason to stay.

Underestimating the art of interviewing

Interviewing is the single most critical phase of hiring. During an interview, you should be able to sense what someone might bring to your company. And this "knowing" can take place within minutes of the interview.

I learned the art of interviewing the hard way or possibly, the only way one can learn anything: through experience.

The first company I worked for as a young adult had the practice of interviewing every person that completed a job application. We believed if this person took the time to fill out an application, they deserved an interview. Often, these interviews would be less than a few minutes, but it was an honorable action and treated the person completing the application as if they were valuable, because they were.

Over the years, I have interviewed well over 5,000 people. Obviously, the vast majority of these interviews did not turn into a hire, so then the goal became to treat them with such respect that they became a customer. And most often, that is exactly what happened.

While your company may have a different structure than the experience I have had, interviewing and hiring is about people. It is about respect, honor, and human behavior. Whether your goal is to convert that applicant into a customer/client or simply an added fan of your business, you have everything to gain in conducting interviews.

If done correctly, every interview is a win. You either gain a great new hire or a great new fan, and that matters in the long run.

The lesson to be learned is no matter what your organization does or who your audience is, interviewing properly can become a valuable resource of business.

I believe in interviewing everyone. To value hiring great people, you must believe in that as well.

It may look different than a physical interview for each person who applies. What matters is the level of engagement you give each person. I have heard more stories than not of resumes being submitted, and no response is given. Your reason for not responding does not matter. The reality the applicant has experienced is they received no response. To them, the story you are telling is that you do not value their effort. That is a major mistake in business. Why? Because people are the lifeblood of any business.

You may be at the level of business that you receive hundreds of resumes and applications for any given position. Each of them deserve a response. In the golden age of automation and technology, there is no reason for your applicants to not receive a response of some sort.

I would greatly encourage you to strategize a plan that allows someone on your team to respond personally. For corporations and larger companies, a personal response may be impossible. I would still encourage you to explore what it would look like if each applicant re-ceived a personal response thanking them for taking the time to ex-plore an opportunity with your company.

Regardless if you implement a personal response system, working through the idea of giving a human, personal touch of engagement with applicants will allow you the space to explore why you are doing what you are doing. The reason many of the challenges you face with employees exist is because you have lost sight of the humanity of your work.

In this culture of automation and technology, we often lose the intima-cy of human connection. But this book is about people. Your life and work should be about people. And if you want to build an organization that lasts, you will learn how to be about connecting, relating to, and empowering people.

That includes someone across the world who may be one of a hun-dred people who applied for a position with your organization. They are still human. And the most honorable action to take is to give them a sincere 'thank-you.'

There are many resources in existence that can give you the generali-ties of interviewing. But nothing can replace sitting across from some-one or looking through a screen at someone or talking on the phone with someone and learning how to read energy, actions, and pres-ence.

Notice I didn't mention learning to read into words or stories or experiences.

Learning the art of listening is needed when interviewing. But even more important is learning to read energy, body language, and engagement. People can tell you anything they desire. They can make up stories or exaggerate experiences or pick and choose all of the good they have done in their life.

But no one can manipulate energy. You can cut it with a knife. Energy, when you learn how to read it, is as noticeable as any words or resume or experience. To be a master interviewer, you must learn to read the presence of energy. You must learn what to notice about someone. You must learn to read body language and eye contact and how to connect the dots between what someone is telling you physically, emotionally, and energetically.

Again, this can most often take place within minutes. Once you learn the art of interviewing the whole person, you will not only raise your awareness of others but also your success in hiring great people.

The key to interviewing lies not only within understanding human behavior but also in understanding the art of question-asking. When you know how to ask the right questions, understand how to connect a response to previous information, and can read the energy of someone, you will be well prepared for hiring people who perfectly align with the role you are filling.

If you have not defined exactly who it is you want filling a role but instead, have spent the majority of your time worrying about the role itself, then it's time to reprioritize how and why you hire.

Any successful business owner understands the value of a target audience. Any great marketing plan has an element of defining that target audience and knowing, without any doubt, who that plan will reach. Often, while creating a marketing plan, agencies will ask their client to physically describe their target.

Who do you want to reach?

What do they look like?

What do they do?

Where do they go?

What do they purchase?

Where do they live?

What are their interests?

These questions lead the client to think more deeply about their message and how they will reach the audience they desire.

This is the same approach you must use when seeking to fill a role in your company.

What type of attitude do you want?

What type of personality will succeed in this role?

What type of thinker will be most advantageous?

Should they be more creative or more analytical?

What type of learner should they be?

Working through this plan and best describing each person you need will give you a huge advantage when hiring. It will save you time, effort, and offer the new person you hire great clarity on what they should be doing and how they are helping build the company.

The more clarity, the more success.

There is an art to hiring.

There is an art to designing your culture.

There is an art to developing people.

Art begins with vision. Vision comes to life with strategy. Strategy takes shape with clarity.

Know who you want to hire, and you are well on your way to building a team of successful people.

Business is art

1- Do you know who you need to hire and why?

2- Which do you currently value more (select one from each choice):

- Skill set or character

- Experience or work ethic

- Past jobs or energy

- Degrees or creativity

3- Who does the interviewing within your organization? Where did they learn to interview? What questions do they ask? When did you review your interview process last?

4- On a scale of 1-10, how do you value your process for interviewing?

5- Does the person or team holding interviews understand how to convert an interviewee into a fan/supporter?

6- Take some time painting the picture of who you want on your team. What hobbies do they have? Where do they hang out? What books do they read? What are they involved in? These are signals as to the type of culture you are creating. You want diversity and strong inclusion on your team- but the basics of each person will have a common thread regardless of their background. Human traits such as positivity, idealism, creativity, work ethic, passion are agnostic to culture, race, ethnicity, or heritage. These are the traits you are clarifying.

CHAPTER 10

We aren't Worried (How you fire people matters)

My heart was pounding in my chest.

I sat back in my chair not sure if what I was hearing was real.

A million questions began running through my mind.

Was this really happening?

Over the years I had fired people. Some because they simply weren't a fit for what I needed. Some because they couldn't do the job. Some because of legalities or crime. I had fired people.

And I hated it every single time.

I believe in compassion. I believe in looking out for the best in each other. I believe that everything in life is connected and no deed goes unanswered. I don't separate business and personal life because I believe life simply is.

This was the second time I had been on the other side of a firing. Both times were from jobs I absolutely loved. They were jobs that, in my mind were fulfilling my childhood dreams. I was doing exactly what I had always desired in life. Both times I was given no real reason.

But this time was different.

A few months before being fired the second time, I was experiencing real burnout. For the first time in my life, I felt a hopelessness and weariness I had never felt. The days and weeks and months and years of running full steam had caught up to me. Added to the internal stress I was feeling was external stress pressed upon me by others. I was working in ministry at the time. The small church I was working with was growing.

The problem with growth is it ushers in a sense of discomfort. The problem with discomfort, especially in areas of faith and decades of systematic traditionalism, is it brings out the worst in people. People feel as if this change you have initiated is a personal attack against not only their belief system but the belief system of their parents and grandparents and great grandparents. This attack of change, in their minds, is an attack on everything they have built and believed in.

Talk about relenting pressure.

My family and I were attacked emotionally, verbally, mentally, and spiritually. Even within a small community, we were made to feel as if we had declared war on this small group of people. While I am grateful for the few who showed love and support during this time, I was mostly scarred from the battles I felt I had to fight.

After months of living with this pressure and unwanted situation, I went to the leadership of the church and asked for some time away. I simply needed a reset. Some time of peace and quiet and a few moments to simply catch my breath.

They supported this idea and agreed to allow me some time away.

Until they changed their mind.

Just three days after the leadership agreed to my sabbatical, they called me in for a meeting. I knew as soon as I walked through the door of that room what was about to take place. I could feel it. There were four men in the room that day. One of them left with his whole world shaken.

I could feel my heart pounding as I sat in the chair across from the other three men. I felt as if I was sitting before a jury and nothing I could say would change the outcome of this event. They showered me with compliments and updated me on discussions they had conducted with other members of that church.

Things were said like 'Mitch you are one of the greatest preachers we have ever heard' and 'you have done more for this little church than anyone we can remember.'

But what has stayed with me through the years more than anything is the last thing that was said to me. It's as if this statement cut through my heart and I have never been able to let it go.

After two of the men had finished speaking, the third made this statement- 'Mitch, we have no doubt you will land on your feet. With your talent and passion, you will be hired in no time and will be well on your way to moving forward. We aren't worried about how you will recover from this.'

At the time, I didn't know how to respond. I was angry. I was hurt. I felt abandoned and let down and like I had failed. This was my dream job. My favorite job to that moment in life.

And now I had been told I wasn't good enough. Or so I thought.

Looking back I can think of a million questions I should have asked. Not that those questions would have brought answers that would have helped. But at least I could have expressed my frustration with what had taken place.

I went over a year without finding full-time work.

It took me well over ten years to recover from losing that job.

It took longer than that for me to recover financially.

If I'm being honest, I still haven't recovered emotionally.

You might have the type of personality that thinks 'Come on Mitch! It's a job. Move on. You can't change it!'

And you're not wrong.

But what I need you to recognize is not everyone has the personality, aptitude, ability to see things as you see. Some of us see things very differently. And if your dream job was ripped from you would you recover that fast?

I doubt it.

I don't care how hard of a personality you have, things impact you. There is something in your life that means so much that if it were taken, it would change you. It may not be a job, but there is something of such great value to you that it guides everything you do in life.

What does this have to do with business? Everything.

> *There is a myth to firing people that needs to be eradicated. That myth? That people respond and recover. Because often, they don't.*

How you fire people matters. What you say to them matters. How you address them and support them and serve them matters.

Maybe you are only about business all the time. Maybe you truly don't care about the people you move on from. If so, you will read this and contemplate what I am offering or you will decide this book isn't for you. I'm okay with that.

But it's possible that compassion still matters in the workplace. That empathy carries more weight in business than revenue and profit. That maybe the larger meaning of humanity has more to do with growth and capitalism and making a dollar.

Hiring and firing people is about compassion. It is about alignment and care and empowerment. It is about simultaneously making sure your company succeeds because it is filled with the people who are working hard to make it succeed.

This is the pivotal ability of great leadership: empowering people to realize they carry the responsibility and reward of a company's success.

Responsibility and reward.

When you view things from this perspective it changes how you fire people. You begin to value even those who weren't able to get the job done or aren't a fit for what you need done. Firing should be done from the heart of compassion. It should be done in a spirit of empathy and understanding.

Take a look at what is taking place when someone is fired:

They are losing provisions for themselves and/or their family.

They are losing a sense of pride.

They might be losing an opportunity to a dream.

They are now fighting a battle of hope.

They have possibly lost benefits.

If someone is fired because of legal issues, we would be telling a different story. But let's focus on the people you choose to fire. The people that may not be who you thought they were or that couldn't get the job done.

In the next few chapters, we are going to look at the possibility of firing and what is the real cause of bringing you to the situation of choosing to fire someone. The cause is in your control more than you realize.

Maybe you have never been fired. Maybe you have absolutely no idea or connection to the idea of being fired.

Maybe you view people who have been fired as losers, failures, or people that simply don't have what it takes to make it in the world of business. I have met many business leaders who feel this way.

Or maybe you have a heart of compassion. Regardless of your situation in the past, you do all you can to relate to the situation at hand. You see others through eyes of empathy and understand that empathy is the doorway to success.

Maybe you relate to my story. That someone, at some point, for little reason, ripped away opportunity from you. Maybe you have spent years building a new world of new opportunities. You have given everything you have to arrive at where you find yourself today. Maybe you're the leader that understands the feeling of being fired so deeply you've invested in becoming a person who has mastered the art of hiring.

Yes- when you fire someone it has everything to do with why you hired them.

So if you want to position yourself in such a way that you can fire people less, then, you must learn the art of hiring. Because most of the people you have to fire can become great employees.

How you fire matters

1- Have you ever been fired from a job? How did you feel? How did it impact your family?

2- What considerations do you take before firing someone? What considerations should you take based on the culture you have designed?

3- What systems are in play to ensure each team member has every opportunity for success?

CHAPTER 11

The Rule of Reflection (The path to great leadership)

Far too many in positions of leadership fail to recognize the most basic principle of leading: The people within your leadership are a direct reflection of you.

The onus of successful leadership lies directly on your shoulders. How your team members respond, function, live, move, and exist is directly related to your ability to empower, inspire, and engage. High functioning leaders are experts at giving the people around them permission to both fail and succeed. As leaders, they take full responsibility when failure takes place and little responsibility when success takes place.

Outside of employees who take part in illegal activity leading to termination, most terminations can be avoided. The percentage of people who deserve to be fired is slim to none, but it begins with leadership. More importantly, it begins with leadership who understands that every single action taking place within their organization begins and ends with them.

As a leader, you are solely responsible for the activities within your organization. Some may argue this idea is an impossibility, that many others also make day-to-day decisions and impact the inner workings taking place. While this is true, as the leader, you have delegated, hired, trained, and approved those in leadership positions within your organization. Therefore, you are responsible. Each decision made by someone else is a direct reflection of your leadership.

I call this the rule of reflection.

Reflection is a critical idea to understand when discussing leadership. It is valuable, because everything that takes place is a direct reflection of leadership. It may be something you have delegated, someone you have promoted, a product that has been introduced, or customer experience. Regardless, every activity, person, and development is a direct reflection of leadership.

Once you understand the rule of reflection, you will then be able to welcome the rule of responsibility. The rule of responsibility is simple:

As the leader, everything begins and ends with you.

This rule in no way gives the leader permission to abuse or overuse their power. The rule of responsibility does just the opposite - it puts the burden of the organization directly on their shoulders. As the leader, you are carrying this burden, and you should carry it well.

Once you understand and accept the rules of reflection and responsibility, you will empower yourself to delegate more appropriately, develop more effectively, and engage more powerfully. You begin to realize that each step you take and each word you speak has influence and power. For the successful leader, the burden of responsibility motivates them to lead with empathy and compassion.

In working with leaders over the years, I have heard many of them place blame on an employee regarding why they didn't last at an organization. While it's obvious that it takes many elements to create a situation, what most leaders miss during these moments of reflection is the opportunity to carry the burden that would ignite growth.

Let's take a look at a few of the top reasons for firing that leaders often give. Each of these reasons places the blame on the employee rather than signifies reflection from the leader.

The employee wasn't a fit.

You hear this often in the world of business. You hear it most often when exploring a company with extremely high turnover. "Not being a fit" for a company has become the easiest and laziest loophole to firing.

But what are you saying when using this reason?

If you will reflect back to earlier chapters of this book regarding hiring, you will remember that one of the single most valuable elements of hiring is alignment. Using the excuse that "someone wasn't a good fit" as your motivating factor for firing them is stating that you hired someone who didn't align from the beginning.

You, or your leaders who you have trained to hire, are the ones who hired this employee. They didn't hire themselves.

So, the underlying issue with this reasoning is you hired the wrong person. You hired a person who simply didn't align with your organization. There are a million reasons for someone not aligning - culture, ideology, philosophy, availability, attitude, aptitude, ability, character. We could go on with reasons someone may not align. Regardless, when you hire someone, you are stating, as an organization, that you believe alignment exists with this person.

Not being a fit is an issue of alignment. Alignment is an issue that is faced during the interview process. While there is a very small percentage of employees you may miss on, rarely should "not being a fit" be the reason for firing someone. This problem should be eradicated during the recruiting and interviewing process.

The employee didn't meet performance standards.

This might be the next most used reason for firing someone that leaders give. Again, it's easy to say someone didn't perform. You may even have the data to back it up. This data becomes your power and measuring stick of success.

But I am here to challenge your performance reason and invite you to reflect on what could have been done to raise performance with this employee.

Anytime a leader says they fired someone because of performance, I raise a few questions that often cause the leader to second guess why they fired this employee at all. If you are ready to be an effective leader, a leader who gives your people every opportunity for success, use these questions to ignite proactive development for your people.

Here are the five questions you must ask when using the reasons of performance as a firing tool:

1- Did you hire the right person for the right job? (Alignment)
2- Who did they train under and why? (Meet with this leader to explore that processes of development and accountability were understood and taught correctly)
3- How did you develop this person during their tenure?
4- Did you repetitively clarify the responsibilities, value, and purpose of this person's role over time?
5- Did this person show any signs of misunderstanding, confusion, lack of knowledge through asking questions, behavior, or performance?

Your responses to these questions are critical to understanding why you fired someone based on performance. If you have hired the right person, placed them in a role that aligns with their ability and aptitude, trained and developed them well, held them accountable, given them permission and empowerment to fail and succeed, partnered with them in communication, and you know that they understand your culture and expectations, you will rarely fire them based on performance.

If you have implemented and performed each of these elements to the best of your ability and the employee continues to underperform, then you will have significant reason to make the change needed.

Outside of legalities, these are the top reasons leaders give for terminating employees. There are many more reasons: Downsizing, economic downturn, shrinking business, tenure, discrimination - which all directly relate to company culture and structure - but for the intent of this book, I want to make this point very clear:

When you decide to fire someone, you are revealing a reflection of yourself, because most terminations that take place can be eradicated through proactive recruiting and hiring or better development and training. It's time to stop blaming employees for being fired and begin taking responsibility for what could have been done more effectively.

As a leader, you want high performers.

As a leader, you want the best team you can build.

As a leader, you want people who represent your company, product, and mission well.

Firing people fulfills none of these desires. It does the opposite. Firing people puts fear in the hearts of your current employees, casts doubt on leadership, and places questions in the minds of your customer base. The worst thing you can do is fire someone. So, you better have legitimate, concrete, beyond a doubt substance for doing so.

When you design a culture of health and understanding, a culture of accountability and growth, a culture of empowerment and alignment, firing someone for good reason is both understood and supported.

But understanding and support can only happen when you live by the two rules of leadership:

The rule of reflection and the rule of responsibility.

Failure to live by these two rules will only cause frustration, burnout, and room for excuses.

I know you are the kind of leader who wants people to succeed. It's time to take responsibility for how that success takes place.

The rule of reflection

1- What does being a leader mean to you?

2- How does this definition impact your daily work?

3- What excuses have you given previously in regard to firing some-one?

4- What process have you implemented to reflect on what led to mak-ing a change with this person?

CHAPTER 12

The Art of Firing (5 steps to ensure understanding, accountability, and conversion)

There are moments when a change must be made. Through culture design, working toward alignment, and using your systems of development, you have provided each of your employees an opportunity to succeed. But sometimes, it simply doesn't work.

People are not stupid. In fact, they are very smart. People tend to know when their time is done and when it's time to move on. There is a story being told each day. Each employee and customer is telling you their story with each step, action, purchase, or investment they make.

The question then becomes: Are you listening?

Are you aware and taking notes on the story being told? This is done through tracking sales activity, notating and reviewing which accounts are performing best, what products clients are purchasing, and when and how leaders are engaging with their team, reviewing performance, etc.

All of these elements make up a larger story being told. Most leaders understand performance review, sales review, analytics, tracking, and data collection, but far too many leaders forget to take note of the larger picture. They often become so caught up in the small actions or details, they forget to step back and see the picture as a whole.

When you fall behind on taking part in and listening to the story, it becomes similar to watching a series on Netflix, only to catch it in season 3 rather than starting from the beginning. Storylines become blurred, you've missed characters that have been written off, and you lost track of how everyone arrived at where they are.

You must start from the beginning. You must keep a record of what is taking place each day.

When you focus on the story at large, following your employees from day one, your knowledge of every employee is now relevant to what is taking place. This is an incredibly valuable action, because now you can measure when it may be time to promote someone, make a change with someone, reward someone, or discipline someone. Without knowledge of the complete story, it is impossible to make any of the needed changes.

The greatest way to pay attention to the story is through systems. We will detail the importance of systems in the next section, but keep in mind that systems are the only possible way to track each part of the story. Systems are also the only possible way to review, reflect, and hold people accountable for their stories.

The story playing out each day is critical when discussing firing someone. To be a compassionate and empathetic leader, you must give people every chance possible to succeed. This is done through systems and accountability. Once you have given someone every opportunity possible to succeed, and they have not done so, it may be time for a change.

The question then becomes: how do you fire with compassion?

Leading with compassion and empathy is the single most sustainable way to grow your organization in every area. Empathy and compassion are always needed, desired, and yield great benefits. Empathy and compassion will never lead you down the wrong path. So, now it is time to learn how to fire with compassion.

Let's explore the five steps to firing someone with compassion. No matter how large or small your business, no matter how many employees you have, you must learn how to use and teach your people to use these five steps.

Remember, once you have decided to fire someone it is now about support and messaging. You want people to leave your company with only good things to say. Sure, being fired is not a small thing. As we've explored in this book, it can literally change people's lives. But it can also become a doorway to success for people. If someone isn't working with your organization, then it's time to guide them to finding an organization where they can be successful.

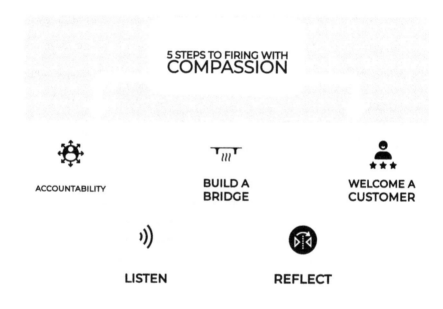

5 STEPS TO FIRING WITH COMPASSION

ACCOUNTABILITY

BUILD A BRIDGE

WELCOME A CUSTOMER

LISTEN

REFLECT

Accountability matters

Firing someone without cause is the laziest way to lead (outside of legalities). To simply decide with no explanation given, no record of support or development, and no guidance for improvement is a reflection of poor leadership. If you have found yourself in this position, then you did your employee a favor by firing them. Because no one should work for an organization that functions this way.

You have worked hard to design a healthy culture, develop systems of operation, and provide a place for success, so you owe it to yourself and your people to hold everyone accountable. Accountability is held through positive affirmation, daily reviews, and permission to act. Everyone on your team is telling a story. Your sole responsibility as a leader is to hold them accountable to the story they are telling.

Accountability is the only thing that gives you permission to both develop or fire someone. You must be consistent in development and accountability. This is important, because once you decide to make a change with someone, as a leader of compassion, you must make sure they understand why this change is being made. There can be no confusion here. This person is about to step into the world, away from your company, and they are going to tell everyone who will listen about their experience. Accountability allows you to support them through this transition.

Learn to listen to their story

Showing up to work on time is telling you a story. Showing up to work late is telling you a story.

Being a good or bad teammate is telling you a story.

Performance is telling you a story.

Passion is telling you a story.

Customer service is telling you a story.

Every single thing that every employee does is telling you a story. If they are not the right person for the job you should know very quickly - If you're paying attention to the story.

If their performance is down you should know why immediately - If you're listening to the story.

As a great leader, you should know, without any doubt, why things are happening the way they are. You should also have a culture so clarified and descriptive that people know when it's not working.

Much of the time, within a culture of accountability and alignment, people will fire themselves. All you will need to do is hold them accountable to the story they are telling.

Build a bridge

Negative experiences always supersede positive experiences. People rarely talk about the positive experiences they've had in life. People always talk about the negative experiences they've had.

Word-of-mouth travels fast. In today's culture, word-of-mouth is now Twitter, Facebook, Instagram, Snapchat, LinkedIn, Youtube, Reddit - we could go on. The point is simple: If you think word-of-mouth traveled fast 10 years ago, then it feels like warp speed in today's climate. Before the door even closes, experiences have been shared with thousands of people.

Because of this, how you fire someone means more today than ever before. You have a choice - that employee can either walk out the door frustrated but appreciative, or they can walk out the door ready to tell the world how you did them wrong.

To be appreciated, all you have to do is listen to the story and build a bridge - a bridge of support - a bridge of trust. A bridge that people are already building themselves; they just simply don't know it.

This isn't about people liking you. This isn't about being soft. This is about being human. It is about becoming aware of how to treat people in the best way possible. Building a bridge of commonality and support is the best way to be human.

Reflect on growth

When you fire someone, it is a common practice to perform exit interviews. Most exit interviews are poorly done, filed away never to be used, and are filled with lies. Who is going to tell the truth when they know nothing will be done? This person is being fired or leaving for a better opportunity for a reason. Why would they disclose their true thoughts and feelings during an exit interview?

There is a way to turn exit interviews into opportunities. This way takes place long before the exit interview is even discussed. This way begins when you recruit the person you are now firing.

A successful exit interview is created from day one. People need to know you are serious about a healthy culture. They need to have experienced the permissive atmosphere you talk about. They need to have seen every opportunity they were given to be successful. When someone knows the truth about your existence, and they know this truth was brought to life through action, they can sit with you at the end of this journey and tell you the truth about what took place.

People need to see that you've taken action, that when previous employees were fired, the information they shared was reviewed, caused reflection, and was put to good use for positive change. When people see this process take place, they will offer their thoughts, even through their last day.

You must reflect on growth. You must admit your mistakes and learn from them. Then, and only then, will you foster a culture of permission and opportunity.

Welcome a customer

If you have done everything within the steps in this book and you still find yourself in that moment of change, it will now be time to welcome a new customer or client to your organization. In other words, you want this person to have had such a powerful experience that they still support your work.

Depending on your company, this support could be through purchases, recruiting other clients, donations, volunteering, or recruiting their friends to work for you. I have personally seen each of these actions taken by someone who was fired. It works. Compassion works. It is possible for you to fire someone, and because of your presence and support, they become one of your greatest fans.

It is also possible to fire someone, and they give a sincere "thank you" when they walk out the door. I have experienced this countless times.

But it only happens when you have the culture we have outlined. When you give every single person every opportunity possible for success, they know when they have failed. They know when it's time to move on. All you have to do is hold them accountable to the story they are telling.

And when you hold someone accountable to their truth, all that's left is gratitude.

If you have to fire people, fire them with compassion. To do anything less is to fail at being a leader.

The art of firing

1- What role does compassion play in your leadership?

2- What systems of accountability have you implemented? When is the last time you reviewed these systems?

3- What actions and words do you take note of daily within your team? How do you respond to what you notice?

4- How do you actively reflect on each day personally and professionally? How would you like to grow in this area? Do you have a partner or friend you can count on to walk with you through this?

5- What process do you use to convert a former team member to a fan/customer/client/supporter?

CHAPTER 13

After They Start (Creating systems to set your team up for success)

The single most undervalued time during an employee's tenure is the very beginning. Most often, too much value is placed on the prerequisites of hiring for the job, education, and experience, leading to the assumption that this new hire will already know much of what needs to take place to do their job well.

This assumption is the mistake many leaders make that kill any chance of success for their employees.

Employees take a job because of the opportunity. They leave because of frustration.

Employees take a job because of money. They leave because of a lack of fulfillment.

Employees take a job because of experience. They leave because there is no room to grow.

Your organization should have such a clear vision for each person, such a strong culture, and such passion for success that every single one of them has no doubt about the path they are on. This clarity and education take place within the first few days of hiring.

The elements of onboarding have become more about signing legalities, explaining benefits, and showing people to their desks. While these are important elements to understanding one's position, it is a minute part of the larger picture.

You must begin to value training and onboarding.
You must design a system for training and onboarding that gives people a real fighting chance at success.
You must create a comprehensive approach to teaching culture above every other element that exist.

If people don't understand your culture, they have zero chance of surviving, much less thriving.

It is possible to drastically lower your turnover by understanding how to hire the right people for your organization. You can lower your turnover even more by training people for success. You can decrease turnover even further by designing a culture of empowerment, alignment, and accountability.

There is no reason why employee turnover or employee frustration can't be but a simple blip on the map of challenges and barriers you face. But the decision is yours.

I want to get you started on creating a system for setting people up for success. While this design tool will be simple, it will certainly have you well on your way to building a system that can, and should, be replicated time-after-time. After working through this system, you will be able to create training programs that will give your people every possible opportunity for success.

This simple system will consist of three elements: logistics, purpose, and culture. Each element is equally important and vital to creating as much clarity as possible during the first week of employment. You want to welcome your new team member with open arms, distinct direction, and immediate success.

This person has committed to building success for you, for themselves, and for those around them. Do not take this investment lightly. They are as invested in helping you succeed as you are. Because they know if they help you succeed, you will help them succeed. That is how great leadership works.

Let's explore the three elements of onboarding and how you are going to implement each element to create success from the start.

3 ELEMENTS OF ONBOARDING

LOGISTICS

PURPOSE

CULTURE

Logistics

- Paperwork
- Introductions
- Benefits
- ID cards
- Parking
- Tour of facilities/office/workspace
- Educational videos
- Digital training

The logistics element of onboarding is often where most organizations stop when bringing a new team member aboard. They fill out paperwork, discuss benefits, show people where to park, introduce them to supervisors, turn on a video or two that they are 'required by law' to show and then tour the office. It's boring at best and, depending on how long the videos are, feels like a waste of a day or two at worst.

You've felt. I've felt it. We have all felt it. The misery of onboarding.

Not that you can get away from legalities, paper work, videos, and tours- you can create a powerful follow up to the logistics element of onboarding that will allow your new team members to feel as if they are taking part in something much more valuable and hopeful.

So fulfill the logistics phase of onboarding as quickly as possible. Let your new team members know early that there are three elements to their first week and logistics is simply one small, but important, part to the plan.

Purpose
- Understanding roles and responsibilities
- Setting up weekly/monthly meetings
- Introduction of accountability system
- Description of expectations and vision
- Performance goals

This is where the fun really begins. The purpose element of onboarding is where you begin to lay the foundation of success for your new team member. This is where you clarify expectations, define their role, help them understand the role of others, and set up measurements for growth and performance.

The power of purpose is found in clarity. When someone knows exactly what they are being asked to do, how they are to accomplish this task, and how they will know when they have succeeded in accomplishing their goal- success is all but a given. But clarity is the key.

So how do you set someone up for success from day one? How do you provide the tools, knowledge and understanding necessary for new team members to thrive?

The answer is simple: clarity and accountability.
Clarity comes when you define someones role by teaching them what they are being asked to do, explaining how they will do it, and setting up a means by which they will measure success or accomplishment.

Accountability comes when you implement systems of teaching, training, learning, and performing. This system fulfills your organizations overall goal, mission, and vision.

Accountability is about more than making sure someone does their job. Accountability is a cultural system in place that ensures everyone understands their purpose and how to fulfill that purpose.

Creating a system for accountability and clarity must be a team effort. Remember, you have developed a culture of inclusion and empowerment so teamwork is of great importance.

This system will consist of three phases: track-ability, timeline, and review. Let's expound on these phases so you have a clear understanding of how to put each into action.

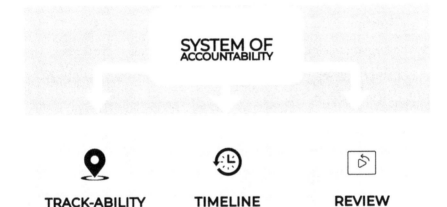

SYSTEM OF ACCOUNTABILITY

TRACK-ABILITY   **TIMELINE**   **REVIEW**

1- Track-ability

The purpose of creating track-ability is to provide clarity regarding your team members role, how they will fulfill their role, and how they will know they have been successful.

To ensure track-ability, you are going to create a training specific to their role that highlights what needs to be accomplished over a given period of time.

It is vital to show the new team member why this schedule is important and how their role and tasks fulfill the greater purpose of your organization. Showing each person how valuable they are to the larger vision is a major step in the direction of employee satisfaction.

2- Timeline

The support pillar to track-ability is setting a timeline of success. This period of time may vary depending on the position but a three, six, nine, and 12 month schedule is a great place to start. Setting a timeline on the front side of tasks and projects immediately creates an opportunity for accountability and follow up. This timeline will help your team members take ownership of their role since you have given them a clear finish line.

While a three, six, nine, and 12 month schedule brings about accountability for the larger vision, you can use this same method for smaller weekly or day to day tasks. The goal is to set a plan of action and accountability through a timeline early so your new team member values this piece of your culture from day one.

Employees want to walk in the door each day knowing exactly what is expected of them and when they need to accomplish each task. Removing any doubt from their minds will allow more energy and space for critical and creative thinking.

3- Review

Within your timeline of success, you are going to include set meetings with each persons supervisor. These meetings must be consistent, scheduled out and standing. Scheduling and honoring meetings with your team will show that you care and are invested in their growth.

During your meetings, spend some time connecting with your employees. Allow them to share how they are doing personally and professionally. These meetings are your opportunity to be human and to relate with each person.

Once you have connected with your team member, review their plan of action and discuss what challenges or barriers they have encountered. Ask if there is anything they need that would equip them to do their job well. Listen to this feedback. Engage at a personal level. Feel their excitement and their frustration. Then set a plan of action to help them succeed moving forward.

The best practice for meetings is weekly. You want to set three meetings each week: leadership team meeting, team member/supervisor meeting, whole team or department team meeting (depending on the size of your organization). These meetings are vital to sustaining your culture and keeping open lines of communication on a consistent basis.

While this is a best practice, don't have meetings simply for meetings sake. No one wants to feel as if their time is being wasted. If you are ready to learn how to facilitate meetings that inspire growth, passion, and performance- send us an email to discuss opportunities where we will teach you how to lead meetings that empower your team: mitch@mitchgraymedia.com

Culture

Educating your team about your culture early is pivotal to creating a culture of sustainability. In other words, you want your culture so deeply embedded within your team and your team so deeply embedded in your culture that it becomes a living, breathing, active energy force.

Team members must be taught what is expected of them and how they can fulfill these expectations in a way that honors the culture you have designed. When culture is empowering and engaging, people will jump at the chance to help their teammate improve and grow. They will also function from honesty so they can hold each other accountable to producing work that fulfills the purpose of the organization.

But culture must be fed. It must be discussed often. Culture must be active, living, and breathing. There are a few things you can do to ensure your culture is getting oxygen each day.

- Create opportunities for team engagement such as group lunches, social outings, or family events. Remember, your employees are human. Expecting them to isolate work life and personal life is an impossible expectation. Embrace the humanity of your people and empower it with connection.

- Develop a small group/mentoring system with your team. This system could consist of partnering a few veteran team members with one or two new team members. Your goal with a small groups systems is to give your veteran team members the opportunity to train and teach new team members about the culture and what is expected of them within their new environment. There is power in veteran team members teaching new team members. It creates instant accountability and ownership and goes a long way in developing sustainable culture.

There are countless ideas as to how you can continue to grow and develop your team. Ask your team members how they would like to improve and continue building a culture of empowerment. You have done all of this work to hire great people! It's time to provide the space for them to be great! If you ask for their ideas, you will be blown away by what they suggest. Listen and put those ideas into action!

Onboarding with vision

1- Take some time to review and describe your current onboarding approach. What is working well? What is not working?

2- Think through what it would take to create and implement an onboarding system containing the elements described in this chapter. What tools, knowledge, training, support would you need to implement this system?

3- How are you currently evaluating your onboarding system?

4- How will you evaluate the effectiveness of this system moving forward?

5- How will you implement ongoing changes needed to improve the process?

6- How will you include the supervisor of a new team member in the onboarding process?

7- How will you include veteran team members in the onboarding process?

8- What steps will you take to develop a small group/mentoring system within your team?

CHAPTER 14

The Parable of James (Why clarity matters)

It was a day like most days. I was setting up my team before heading out, empowering them to help guests and finish the action list for the day while making sure to offer the best service possible.

My closing manager (James) was following up to make sure he understood what needed to be accomplished, and I specifically pointed out some branding and merchandising that needed to be done with the new product we received earlier in the day. He specifically asked if I had any ideas, desires, or thoughts on the task. I blatantly stated, "I will leave that up to you. Just make sure we highlight the new product!"

I gave high fives on the way out the door and went home satisfied with how I left my team for the evening.

The next day, I arrived at my store, took my walk around, and noticed the project that had been finished by James the previous night. It was not at all what I wanted. Was it poorly done? No. Was it blatantly against what I requested? No. Did he do his best with the instructions he had been given? Yes.

But I was not satisfied.

I spent half the day undoing his work and displaying the product as I saw fit. Later that evening, James arrived for his shift and immediately asked, "Why did you change my work? I did what you asked." Stumbling through some words and thoughts, I tried to explain why I didn't like his effort and that it needed to be redone.

I never apologized.

I never asked questions to better understand why he set up the product the way he did.

Instead, I proceeded to tell him he didn't do things correctly, so I had to redo his work.

I will never forget his following statement:

"Mitch, don't ever ask me to merchandise again. If you do, I will say no. If you want to fire me, fire me. But I will never do something you ask if you're simply going to tear down the work I did."

He was right.

I never clarified exactly what I wanted. I never asked him to explain his vision to me. I never asked for his input or ideas. I simply asked him to merchandise the new product. That was it. And he did just that.

James worked with me for another two years following that incident. He became one of the best employees I have ever had. And he never merchandised a wall again.

James taught me a few things during that incident. These lessons have become principles over my decades of leadership. They are principles that every leader should follow to create an environment of success and empowerment.

When you lack clarity in defining jobs, projects, roles, and responsibilities, you relinquish your ability to hold people accountable.

It is impossible to hold someone accountable for something they do not know or understand. Yet far too many leaders give little clarity and show anger or disappointment when their employees meet the standard of lack of clarity.

The responsibility of clarity lies on the shoulders of those in leadership positions. Period. There is no in-between or indecisiveness here. As a leader, it is solely your responsibility to provide clarity for each of your employees.

Accountability only matters when it is stated, not assumed.

This may surprise you, but not a single person under your leadership has the ability to read minds. It doesn't exist. Assumptions are the enemy of greatness and success. You cannot thrive when you live by the rule of assumption.

To have the right to accountability, you must provide clarity of vision, clarity of responsibility, and clarity of expectation. Each of your employees must understand these three areas of their role without any doubt. In a highly functioning environment, not only do employees understand these three areas about their role, but they also understand these three areas regarding every other person's role.

Everyone understands the part they are to play as well as the part everyone else should be playing. This is how highly successful organizations function. This should be your goal as well.

If you pay attention, your employees will make you a much better leader.

One of the greatest acts you can participate in, especially as a leader, is to overcome ego. We all deal with it - thinking too highly of ourselves, thinking too little of others, thinking we are better than those around us. This is especially prevalent when you are in a position of hiring, developing, and signing your name on the bottom of others' paychecks.

Pride can often get in the way of learning. Pride is the opposite of learning. The path of learning is only available through the door of humility. To become a leader of compassion and empathy, you must be constantly learning, growing, evolving. You must stay curious about the things and people that can challenge your current state of being.

Unfortunately, many leaders forget this perspective of life. They arrive at a certain position and suddenly feel as if they are in control. The reality is you are never in control. You cannot control the thoughts, actions, words, or evolution of others. There will always be people in the world who have more knowledge, experience, or talent than you.

As a leader, you are much better served listening, studying, and asking for the feedback of your employees. Listen to them. Honestly receive the things they say or questions they ask. This transparency and humility will go a long way in building the relationships needed to fulfill the vision of your company.

Ask how you could have done it better.

Anytime I see a leader who asks their people how they can be a better leader, I see someone who truly understands and appreciates the position of leadership. You are being entrusted with the thoughts, emotions, and well being of others. To think you have all of the answers, to have the audacity to hold someone accountable for something you have not clarified, or to change the work of an employee behind their back is cowardice at best.

You are human.
They are human.

You are no better because of your position or power.

They are no less because they work "for you."

They don't owe you anything.

You owe them everything.

Understanding this is the difference between a great leader and someone who simply has the title of leader.

Leading to your potential

1- Reflect on a time you did not communicate as clearly as you should have. What were the ramifications of this miscommunication? What would you have done differently? What have you learned from that moment?

2- Great leadership is founded on vulnerability and honesty. How could you improve on being more vulnerable with your team?

3- How have you given employees the opportunity to share honest feedback with you?

4- How do you respond to this feedback and how has it helped you grow as a leader?

5- When is the last time you asked your team how you could be a better leader? Are you willing to ask this question now?

6- How will you use the response of your team to help you grow?

CHAPTER 15

Leading with Heart

There is this myth among many leaders that their role is to be hard, tough, and distant - the idea that they are the disciplinarian and judge sitting atop a perch looking down on their employees.

Let's be honest, this is a slave master mentality. It is a mentality that shows others you think you are better than they are. That you are the one in control. You are the first and last. The beginning and end of their professional lives.

The truth is - you are none of these things.

You may hire someone, but they choose to work for you.
You may pay someone, but they expend energy on building the revenue to "earn" that paycheck.
You may have a title of power, but every single one of your employees, customers, and clients can choose to not work with or for you on any given day.

You could lose every ounce of power you have earned in a second. You are not in control.

So, how do you lead once you come to this realization? You learn to lead with heart.

The greatest asset you have as a leader is your humanity. People want to know your story. They want to connect with you in a way they can understand. They want to see your humanity at a level they can relate to. This can be done by engaging with employees on a personal level, taking interest in their lives, families, and endeavors.

One of the greatest actions a leader can take is to show interest in the passions of employees. Every single person who works with you has interests outside of work. Are they taking classes to finish a degree? They could be creating a side hustle to make some extra money. Maybe they are coaching their child's little league team. Ask about these things. Support them in any way possible. Make sure they know you want to be sincerely connected on a human level.

When you lead from a place of humanity, you create the opportunity for connection.

People value the human story. They value the ability to connect with you through compassion and empathy. Leading with heart means you create an environment that places relationships before revenue and people before profit. Organizations that create this type of environment are setting them up for not only success but the sustainability of that success.

Functioning from your humanity as a leader causes the greatest trickle down effect that exists. Your employees reflect and mimic how they are treated. In treating your people with kindness, you are also showing them how they must treat customers and clients. As a customer, when someone creates a negative experience at a business, you can be sure they are simply reflecting how they are treated. Conversely, when you have a positive experience, you can be sure this positivity is a direct reflection on leadership.

I was visiting with someone recently who has a background in leadership, working for major corporations as well as being incredibly successful in building companies herself. We were in a small group setting, and the topic of the conversation turned to the idea of showing gratitude in the workplace. This conversation and my new friend's response sheds light on what is missing within many organizations.

One of the people in this meeting asked a very pointed question: "Mitch, how do you think I can apply this idea of expressing gratitude during my time at work?"

This is a great question. My response was simple - leaders in the workplace must become more aware and intentional with creating space and time for their employees to intentionally express gratitude. I also mentioned that employees can take more initiative in taking action on moments of gratitude. The person who asked the question then began to explore the idea of what it would look like for her, as an employee, to propose to her leaders the idea of taking time to express gratitude regularly during meetings.

As we vocalized our curiosity, my new friend with a background in corporate business spoke up and shared some reflections regarding her time in the corporate world. She expressed her frustration about how so many leaders do not leave room for gratitude. She also shared her experiences in corporate business meetings where everything is cut and dry, action-oriented, and creates zero space for gratitude or joy.

This firsthand example is what losing the humanity of leadership looks like. When you leave no space for people to express their humanity, gratitude, frustration, joy, or hope, you will soon find yourself sitting in the room alone, and no one following your vision any longer.

Humanity is meant to live together. Humans are built to show the expression of feelings and emotions. There is no shortcut when dealing with this part of your work. As a leader, you have intentionally decided to take on the responsibility of leading other humans. While you may have your job description to fulfill while you are tasked with growing or improving your organization, you are given the challenge of holding people accountable. Your single, overarching goal as a leader is to better the lives of those you lead.

At the end of the day, if you call yourself a leader, and you cannot identify how you made those under your leadership better, then you are no leader. You may have the title. You may have the salary. You may even be celebrated in some circles as being a good leader. But when you look your people in the eye and cannot honestly say you have made their lives better, you are not a great leader.

The most interesting thing about leading from the heart is it doesn't take much time or effort. Regardless of the size of your organization or how valuable your meetings are, you can take a few minutes out of each meeting to express gratitude. You can take 20 minutes a day to personally thank your people for the work they do. In the age of technology, there is absolutely no reason you cannot be expressing gratitude and encouraging your people daily.

There are no more excuses. All that is left is a choice - to lead with heart or to ignore the humanity of leadership.

The most sustainable way to increase revenue isn't more product. It isn't an improved product. It isn't more marketing or expanding market places.

The single most sustainable path to increased revenue is creating a great experience.

The single most effective way to a great experience is connecting with and empowering your people.

The single most impactful way to connect and empower is to lead with heart.

Empowering your team

1- How could empowering leadership impact growth, productivity, and profit?

2- Do you believe leadership is a great responsibility?

3- How does viewing leadership as a responsibility change the way you view your work?

4- Have you considered that your role as a leader impacts the lives of others? How does this make you feel? How does this view of leadership shape your view of your job?

5- In five sentences or less, describe the type of leader you would like to be.

6- From the description you have developed, set five steps of action you will take to begin growing into the leader you would like to become. These steps could include actions such as reading books on leadership, hiring a leadership or personal development coach, or asking your team for feedback.

CHAPTER 16

Give them a Reason to Stay

As you have seen throughout this book, the data is very clear -

People take jobs for money, but they don't stay for the money.

This is a principle of human behavior regarding work that is proven year after year, decade after decade, time after time.

You can pay someone all of the money in the world, but the story tells us that if their experience is heart-wrenching, and the environment is emotionally mutilating, they will not stay.

I can recall multiple situations throughout my management career when I offered one of my top performers a raise, yet they still chose to move to another company. And it was never for the money. Looking back, I can pinpoint the exact reason these high performers chose to move on: I was not offering them the experience nor opportunity they deserved.

Like anything in life, you will never get it right every single time. But there is a way you can get it right the majority of the time. This is very true when it comes to recruiting, hiring, developing, and retaining great people in your organization.

Before you can begin to develop and retain great people, you have to reflect on the culture you have designed, the systems you have implemented, and the process of growth and opportunity you are building. People are very smart. They can easily take a look across the landscape of your organization and identify what opportunities lie before them.

You often hear of organizations that don't promote the people who truly deserve a promotion. Rather, they promote employees who have tenure or are friends or who make the most noise about the promotion. Other employees take note of each of the situations, and they do not forget.

Employees keep score of everything you do, good or bad.

They notice who you hire.
They notice who you promote.
They notice who gets the opportunities and who doesn't.
They notice who you interact with consistently.

Employees take note of everything. So, you must be transparent, understanding, and create an environment of true equal opportunity for all, not just a few.

We are talking about giving people a real reason to stay with your organization, a reason that justifies their energy investment into your greater vision.

As a leader, your first goal is to design a culture that is empowering, welcoming, and challenging. Next, you must find people who align with this culture and mission (recruit). Third, you must have a system of development and accountability that gives these people not only permission to succeed but also permission to grow. Lastly, you must create a culture of opportunity.

Humans have an innate desire to be part of something much larger, much greater, much more meaningful than what is taking place within their own lives.

Your final task as a great leader is to create a vision, mission, and system so clear and full of opportunity that everyone understands why they show up each day.

Clarity for employees.
Clarity for customers.
Clarity for partners.
Clarity for owners.

Clarity in life makes everything work to its optimum purpose and potential.

Employees simply want to know that you care, more than just about little Johnny's baseball game or Sarah's recital. That matters incredibly, but they want to know that you also care about their evolution in life. They want to know that this relationship between employee and boss means more than just being told what to do and signing paychecks.

Human behavior shows us that we all crave value. And really, we all need to know we are valued.

You know this in life outside of work. You would never stay in a relationship where you were not valued. You, as a leader, would never work for a boss who showed zero value to their people. You would never allow your child to play on a team where they were not valued. You would never take part in a community where you were not shown value.

Great leaders understand this principle of life so deeply, they apply it to the workplace. And because of this high value-driven culture, they nurture and grow leaders.

The greatest way to show value and give people a reason to stay is to design a culture where everyone is a leader.

Everyone has a clear responsibility.
Everyone holds someone accountable and is held accountable.
Everyone is a vital part of breathing life into the greater vision.

Everyone engages others daily and leaves at the end of the day, knowing something important took place.

Everyone understands the value and importance of every single task - no matter how large or small.

Everyone understands they are an incredibly important piece to building success.

There are a million ways to show value to your people. Some are small, consistent ways that take place often. Some are larger ways that may be designed to reward those who have invested more than others. Regardless of how you show value, you must design a specific strategy for showing this value consistently - a strategy that will hold yourself and your team accountable moving forward.

Understanding why they stay

1- What steps have you implemented that give people every opportunity possible to not only succeed, but thrive?

2- What is your system for promotion? How could you improve this system where everyone has an opportunity?

3- Why do you stay with your organization?

4- Why do you think others stay?

5- What exists within your organization that would motivate someone to stay?

CHAPTER 17

Fear: The Great Teacher

Our culture does not understand fear. We are about to change that.

Like many, I was raised in a culture that taught one thing about fear: It was the enemy.

We prayed fear away. We ran from fear. We ignored fear. We yelled at fear. But then, we were faced with fear.

Maybe it was a high school coach who believed in using fear as a motivational tactic, or a pastor who screamed and yelled from the pulpit each Sunday to scare the hell out of you. Sometimes, it was an elementary school teacher, who swatted your hand with a ruler, so you would obey her demands.

We were told fear was the enemy. Then, it was used as a motivator?

Nothing about that makes any sense at all.

Here is the truth about fear: It is a great teacher.

Fear is a natural tendency within all living beings. From humans to animals to children to adults to leaders to employees. Everyone knows fear. Everyone experiences fear. So, there is no way, by natural order, that it is an enemy.

We are the ones who have made fear an enemy, when all along, fear is actually a friend.

Fear teaches us to listen, to be more aware.
Fear teaches us to reflect on our mistakes, so we can learn from them.
Fear empowers courage - the courage to move forward even in the midst of the unknown.
Fear guides us to greater knowledge of self - the knowledge that will lead us to growth and maturity.

By nature, fear is not a manipulator or deceitful or demanding. Fear is neutral. It exists. We own the power of response to fear.

So, what does fear have to do with leadership? With hiring? With developing great people?

Everything.

Many leaders believe in a bullying approach to leadership, the type that is belittling, insulting, voice-raising, obnoxious, and highly unsustainable. What follows this kind of leadership concerning employees is very high turnover, low job satisfaction, and often volatile performance. A bully in leadership never works.

Some leaders take a passive-aggressive approach. They never quite give their people the greater clarity needed to create sustainable success. They rarely provide an opportunity for growth and often use nondescript tactics in holding others accountable or in defining responsibility. Similar to the bully, passive-aggressive leaders feel the need to hold total control over every situation.

Both of these types of leadership believe in fear as a tactic for motivation. But if we look deeply, if we look through the eyes of compassion, what we see are people who are driven by fear themselves. They often fear transparency, because transparency calls for us to deal with our shadow selves - the part of us we would often rather keep dormant.

The fear-driven leader is also often driven by false pride. They believe if they grow and nurture people, someone may become better at their job than they are and take it from them. To defend against this made up scenario, the leader operates from a position of manipulation, oppression, and negativity. Constantly making sure others know that the leader's job is not up for grabs.

Once you understand the deeper concept of what is taking place within these types of leaders, it better prepares you to either function around them, teach them, leave them, or not become them. The choice they have made is to allow fear to drive them in a negative way that hides the real issues at hand.

But fear can teach us how to become great leaders.

The humble, empowering, compassionate leader will listen to fear. They believe in empowering others to the extent that those around them become better leaders than themselves. This is the real measurement of a great leader: They continuously nurture even greater leaders.

The leader who becomes the student of fear understands the power of reflection, humility, and empathy.

Fear may say, "you are not good enough." The great leader will respond, "show me where I can grow."

Fear may say, "they are better than you." The great leader will respond, "help me focus on myself and how I can do all I am capable of."

Fear may say, "why do you think you can lead people?" The great leader will respond, "I am no different from anyone else, but I am ready for the challenge at hand."

The great leader understands the complicated state of the human spirit yet learns, listens, and submits to the teachings of fear.

The great leader has an innate desire not only to lead but to be led, thus positioning themselves as a student first.

The great leader knows the impact of constantly learning, reading, evolving, and changing, so they may always be walking the path of curiosity.

What makes a leader great is not the number of people following. It is the permission and empowerment they bestow on those around them.

Fear may be the greatest teacher you learn from. Fear can teach you what you are doing well while also permitting you to learn something new. Fear can take your moments of doubt and turn them into water-shed moments of full belief.

You can become a great leader. The beautiful reality of leadership is your greatness is not measured by the greatness of others but rather, by the greatness you allow yourself to become.

A student of fear

1- How has fear guided you in the past?

2- What are some moments, within your leadership experience, where you allowed fear to dictate your actions?

3- How could you use the idea of becoming a student of fear to empower your team members?

4- What are five lessons you can learn from fear today?

5- How do you need to shift your perspective of fear?

CHAPTER 18

Healthy People Make Healthy Employees

While society has come a long way in addressing mental health, we still have such a long way to go. There is no doubt that the conversation about mental health has become much more inviting and available. But there remain opportunities to improve our efforts in providing support, healing, and a safe space for those who deal with mental health issues.

When we consider the battle surrounding mental health, the reality has to become clear: We all struggle with mental health at some level. For some, this level is small and minute. It might simply be the battle of self-talk or days, few and far between, where you may feel down or less than normal. For others, the battle of mental health is everlasting and often becomes more difficult by the day. It might be a struggle with depression, anxiety, PTSD, or a myriad of other causes. The days of darkness, for many, arrive often. A single day, or even moment, of respite, is a welcome surprise.

Ignoring these issues causes much more harm than good. Many have been raised in a culture where they learned that mental health struggles are a myth; it is simply something that can be solved through hard work or focus or prayer or eating better. These schools of thought could not be further from the truth. There are many paths one can take to equip themselves in coping with mental health. But for many, this battle will be an ongoing journey that might last their entire life.

So, how does a leader provide support in the workplace when it comes to mental health? How do you create a culture and environment of acceptance, understanding, and empathy, balanced with progress, growth, and productivity?

Let's take a look at some key data that will help guide you in designing a workplace culture that is safe, productive, and inspires positivity.

- Strong office design can make employees up to 33% happier at work
- 1 in 6 workers experiences common mental health problems including anxiety and depression
- Happy employees experience 31% higher productivity
- Happy employees take fewer sick days and stay in their role twice as long
- 77% of employees feel that a flexible work schedule aids in productivity
- The average person spends a third of their day in the workplace

The bottom line is simple: The happier your employee, the more productive and committed they become.

Recruiting is valuable.

Hiring people that align with your culture, mission, and role is of utmost importance.
Providing clarity through development is immeasurable.

But the single most important thing you can do for your people is to provide a culture and atmosphere where they feel comfortable, welcomed, and empowered. This is what happiness in the workplace looks like.

We know many people struggle with mental health. You have people working with your organization who struggle with mental health. You, a business leader and decision-maker, may even struggle with mental health. This is the reality of life. It is a part of humanity that is present and unavoidable.

As a leader, you have the decision to design a culture that empowers and supports people or not. There is no in between. You are either providing a place of support and positive impact, or you are avoiding the situation. You cannot be inconsistent concerning this subject. You must decide on your path and commit.

If you want increased productivity, you will focus on designing a culture of health.

If you want people to commit to your organization, you will focus on designing a culture of health.

If you want better customer/client relations, you will focus on designing a culture of health.

If you want to increase revenue and grow your organization, you will focus on designing a culture of health.

Healthier, happier, positive people will grow your business. And they will love doing it, because they know you support them.

How do you design a culture of health concerning mental health specifically? Here are five ways to immediately provide support and opportunity for anyone battling mental health issues.

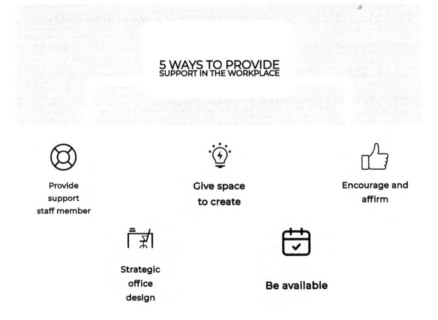

5 WAYS TO PROVIDE
SUPPORT IN THE WORKPLACE

Provide
support
staff member

Give space
to create

Encourage and
affirm

Strategic
office
design

Be available

Provide a support staff member who will offer support.

If you can hire a counselor or therapist within your organization, do so.

If you cannot hire a licensed counselor or therapist, explore hiring a certified life coach, personal development coach, or a certified facilitator.

If you are not able to hire any of these, explore the possibility of getting certified as a facilitator yourself or having one of your team members become certified. Becoming a facilitator is very inexpensive and will allow your team to have support when they need it.

Regardless of how you have to make this happen in the present, do what you can. Create a working support group, take a class on becoming a facilitator, partner with a counselor at your local college or university to work part-time for you or to teach you the basics of listening and supporting others. There are many solutions and possibilities. Many of which cost little to nothing.

The focus is to simply take action at whatever level you can. This action will show your people that you are serious about designing a culture of health and will support them as they need it.

Office design matters

Strong office design can drastically influence the mentality of your people. No one enjoys working in a dark, dingy, musty, unwelcoming place. We enjoy light, openness, and privacy when needed but also community when needed.

Make sure your workspace is welcoming and inviting. The more natural, outdoor light, the better. Use plants and art to inspire life and thought. Challenge your employees to get outside as often as possible. If you're able, design workspaces outside, so people can enjoy the outdoors and work simultaneously.

Design a workplace health challenge. This can be done through walking clubs or workout challenges. You can also create policies and practices that shape a culture of health. This might look like removing vending machines that are filled with high sugar products and replacing them with water and fresh produce offerings.
Design spaces of work that invite people to work at their best.

Give people the space to create

One of the most underrated negative actions a leader can take is to be overbearing. People will not work for an overbearing leader for long. Being controlling, rude, or passive-aggressive can ruin best-laid plans quickly.

When you give someone a task, after you have clarified their purpose and job, give them room to work. They will make mistakes. Use these moments to help them fail forward and grow. Encourage your people to make mistakes! Celebrate these mistakes as moments of growth and learning!

The most effective way to help your people feel empowered is to trust them with their work. When they know you trust them, their performance will grow exponentially.

Be available

When leaders are absent, work falters.

When leaders are positively present, work soars.

You may be the owner, CEO, manager, department head, team leader - regardless of your title, you're reading this book, because you are a leader or desire to be one.

If I had to give you one single piece of advice on how to be a great leader, it would be this:

Be actively, positively present.

Your team needs to see you each day or as often as possible. They need to interact with you and relate to you. They need you to sincerely ask about their family and how the baseball game or birthday party or recital went. If you're an incredible leader, you will do all you can to potentially attend an event every once in a while. Attend a graduation or religious service or an activity with your people.

Your employees need to see that you are human. Too many leaders miss this critical part of leadership.

Yes, you are their "boss." Yes, you hold them accountable. Yes, you may give them their paycheck. But when all they know about you is you are watching their back and criticizing their every move, you will soon see them moving out. For good.

Get your hands dirty by working alongside them. There's a reason everyone loves watching the TV show "Undercover Boss." Because as most people are watching, they are thinking, "now that boss sees what we go through every day." And boss's are thinking "wow, I never knew what they went through every day!"

Be human. Be relatable. Be present.

Encourage and affirm

Positive reinforcement always makes more impact than negative rein-forcement. No one enjoys being yelled at. No one enjoys being re-buked. No one enjoys negativity.

When you see someone doing a nice job, tell them! When you see someone struggling, let them know you are there, ask how you can help, and let them know they will get through it.

Spend your time encouraging and affirming.

If you're a leader who fears affirming your people, get over it. That's a reflection of you, not a reflection of how affirmation makes others feel. Affirmation makes people feel strong; it gives them pride that they have done well, and it empowers them to do well again and again and again.

This idea that affirmation makes people soft or perform worse is a myth. In no way can it be proven. Numerous studies throughout the years have shown that affirmation does just the opposite. It motivates people to work harder, learn more, and grow. Affirmation shows your people that you see them and believe in them.

Seeing and believing is always a good thing. Every single time.

Begin exploring how you can implement these steps right away. You may not be able to hire a certified counselor or coach, but you can begin affirming your people now. You may not be able to remodel your space, but you can purchase a few plants, move some desks around, and begin a walking club. There are steps you can take today to improve the health of your people. And the result of improved health is greater performance and commitment.

Health matters

1- How has your organization addressed creating an environment of health for your employees?

2- What steps have you taken to ensure your team members have opportunities to grow, heal, and be supported?

3- What ideas mentioned in this chapter would you like to consider implementing within your organization? What other ideas have you considered or would like to consider?

4- What changes could you make immediately to support your employees health physically, emotionally, mentally, and spiritually? What tools would you need to take these steps? Who needs to be involved?

5- How is your health? Stop for a few minutes and take honest inventory of each area in your life. After all, it takes a healthy leader to lead healthy people.

How is your physical health? How are you caring for yourself in this area?

How is your emotional health? How are you investing in this area?

How is your mental health? What steps are you taking to grow and evolve mentally?

How is your spiritual health? Who are you learning from? How are you empowering the deepest parts of your humanity?

CHAPTER 19

Bringing the Art of Humanity Back to Leadership (5 ways to impact your team today)

It all began with a simple 'How are you?'

I was making my normal weekly rounds to touch base with each team member on my team at the time and felt an energy with a specific teammate that was a bit outside their norm. So I looked this team member in the eye and asked, 'How are you?'

He looked away, put his hands in his pockets and verbally danced around the question in hopes I wouldn't notice.

I stopped him and this time asked, 'No-really- how....are....you?'

As soon as I finished the question his eyes filled with tears, his face flushed and it seemed as if his body had been hit with a thousand pounds. We found a more private place to visit and he shared with me some of the struggles he was currently facing. Some were of his own demise. Some were outside of his control. Regardless, life was incredibly difficult during this season and he simply needed someone to listen.

So I did. For over an hour.

After our conversation you could immediately feel the change in his disposition. He was closer to his usual self. His troubles hadn't suddenly disappeared. He knew what he had to face once he left for the day. But for that moment and for the next seven hours, he could focus on the task at hand because someone cared enough to listen.

As I've stated multiple times throughout this book- it is impossible to segregate and separate work life and personal life. Impossible. Regardless of how much energy one might put into compartmentalizing life, it just doesn't work.

Your team members are living this life just as you. They work. They play. They have hobbies and bills and kids and families and side hustles and interests and favorite TV shows and passions and pastimes and hopes and dreams. You cannot remove those elements of life once they walk through the door of your organization.

So as a leader, you have a decision to make: embrace all of their humanity or continue to hide from the fact that humans are, well, human.

A great leader embraces the fullness of humanity. Great leaders are compassionate, sincere, interested, and engaged. Personal issues don't scare great leaders. Human challenges don't place fear in the hearts of great leaders. Maybe you've never considered becoming a great leader. That's okay. If not, just become a kind human. Because kind humans are great leaders.

So how do you fully embrace the humanity of your team? How do you balance the fact that life happens with productivity within your organization? It is possible, and even-more, it is empowering.

Let's discuss five ways to impact your team today in a way that will show them you care, your good intention, and your hope for their success.

Ask each team member what they enjoy about their work

Such a simple thought yet amazingly, so few ask this of their team members. Asking each person what they enjoy about their work accomplishes two things:

- It shows each person that you truly want to know how they relate to their work and why it brings them joy

- It gives you feedback about each person you would not find otherwise.

When you ask someone what they enjoy about something they will often share insights to their dreams, thoughts, and imagination. This information is invaluable when aligning your team with work that allows them to operate at full potential.

You may have someone in a position that they perform well but don't enjoy. You may have a need in another area that this person would align with best but if you never ask, you may never know!

Asking questions such as this open doors of opportunity that are impossible to open when you simple hand out tasks and demands and deadlines.

Ask each team member to share the greatest challenge they face with their work

One of your most important missions as a leader is to put your team in position to step into success. Knowing and understanding each person's greatest challenges allow you to gauge how well they have been trained but also allows you to measure the job at hand.

I often see people placed in a position simply because they are willing yet are never equipped for this new position or work.

> *Willingness is amazing, but willingness is simply frustration wrapped in a positive attitude when people are not equipped to do their work well.*

Ask each team member how they are doing- personally

I began this chapter with a real story of what it looks like to lead from your humanity. Often, people will talk about leadership as if it is militaristic and solely founded on authoritarianism. But that isn't great leadership.

While there are as many ways to lead as there are humans walking the earth, there are also ways not to lead. Some of those ways include insulting others, belittling others, bullying, screaming, talking down to others, and ignoring the humanity of others. These tactics are, in no way, included in how a great leader acts, lives, moves, speaks, and breathes.

When you take the time to ask someone how they are doing and intentionally listen to them, you are creating the space and permission for the other person to be fully human. You are telling them that it is okay to step into their emotion, frustration, hurt, celebration, or anger. Those are all very positive emotions and states of being. They are a part of being human.

Many people in leadership positions give the excuse that they don't have time to deal with other people's problems. I have personally heard leaders and owners use phrases such as 'I don't run a counseling service here' or 'I'm not a therapist. Deal with that on your own time.'

While these owners/leaders may not be totally wrong about their statements, they are wrong regarding their perception of their employees.

You better be listening to and caring for your employees. If you don't, they will soon go somewhere where they are accepted and heard. And they should.

Your lack of humanity is not their fault. It's yours. And my guess is if you have a problem of high turnover among your team, you also have a listening problem as well. Each team member is telling you exactly what they need to succeed. The question is- are you paying attention?

Take this feedback to heart and do something about it

Many are great at asking for feedback. Few do anything with it.

It's time to review your plan of action in relation to the feedback your team is giving you. What are you doing with each of those surveys and exit interviews? What plan do you have to do something with the feedback you are given?

Similar to the plans of action we have outlined for your team within this book, you also need to develop a plan of action that will empower the feedback your team is giving you. This feedback is both verbal and nonverbal.

The most important rule to sincere leadership is simple: When they speak, listen. After you listen, act.

Say 'Thank you'

The two most undervalued words in the English language are 'Thank you.' We don't say it enough. More importantly, we don't show it enough.

A few years into my first leadership role I began a practice that I've done my best to use over the past 20 years. I began this practice after telling someone 'thank you' for coming to work one day. They looked at me and stated 'Mitch, I have to come to work.' I responded with 'no you don't. You don't have to do anything. But you chose to come to work. You made the conscious effort to get dressed, get in your car, and come to work. No one made you do that. So thank you.'

They were dumbfounded. I have used this approach to gratitude toward others with other professionals, with high school students, with athletes, with my own children, and with myself. It works. When someone gives you a sincere 'thank you,' your spirit soars.

Gratitude is the key to an open heart- for yourself and for the one you are sharing gratitude with.

Share a simple 'thank you' at the end of each day with your team. Thank them individually for something specific they did that day. Be sincere. Be meaningful. Share the emotion you feel knowing this team of people are helping build your success.

Gratitude can take a difficult day and turn it into gold. Because gratitude is the key to an open heart and open mind.

Gratitude is the key

1- How have you struggled with listening to your employees in the past?

2- How would you like to be a better listener moving forward?

3- How can you provide a space that allows your team members to live within their full humanity?

4- Take some time to define what gratitude means to you. List five things/people you are grateful for.

5- How can you use gratitude to daily empower your team?

CHAPTER 20

The Power of Interpersonal Growth

Humans, by nature, are spiritual beings.

We are beings that are filled with complication and thought and change and find ourselves ever-evolving over time.

But a crazy thing often takes place when change occurs- we get frustrated!

I remember the first time I heard someone make the statement 'well, that's how it's always been here and how we've always done it!' At the moment, I wasn't sure how to respond. But that moment is definitely one I wish I could revisit and have a different kind of conversation with the person who made that statement.

The troubling part, this person was in a leadership role, unwilling to change, and unrelinquishing in their quest to hold to the traditions and beliefs of the past.

So what does spirituality and holding to tradition and hiring people and running an organization and recruiting and humanity have to do with interpersonal work and success?

Well- as you've read throughout this book when I ask such a question- the answer is.....

EVERYTHING!

You are sitting with this book either because you are curious about how to hire and keep great people or you are struggling to keep the people you hire or you sincerely want to become a better leader or all of the above.

But before you can begin to unravel the issues you are facing outside of yourself, you must first face the challenges and issues taking place within. We all have them- those unrevealed thoughts and emotions and inner conversations that make us doubt ourselves and those around us. No one has it figured out. Some are better at practicing the art of self- work but no one is perfect.

And that is perfectly okay.

I want to close this book with a thought, and a challenge. I want to help you draw a line of connection between the challenges you are facing within your organization to the challenges you are facing internally. Because they are connected.

After all, what is taking place outside of you is simply a reflection of what is taking place within. And this news, my friend, is good news. Why? Because if what is taking place outside of you is a reflection of what is taking place within then that means you have the power to change that reflection by doing the work within yourself.

And that is the power of humanity: you control the reflection.

Admit it- you always check the mirror after you get a haircut, take that first shower, wash and style your hair. Everyone does. And it...looks... good.

Life is much like that reflection after that fresh cut and style. You FEEL it. In fact, you feel it so much that you get dressed up and find a reason to go out that evening. There's a strut to your stride and style in that smile because you not only know you look good, you know you feel good.

The question becomes- what made you feel so good? Are you a different person than you were before the haircut, style and outstanding outfit? Are you a different person than you were 24 hours ago?

No.

But a reflection has power. A reflection can show you what you want to see or it can show you the truth of what truly exists. The power of this reflection, though, is in our choice of what to see.

The same can be said for what is taking place within your leadership. You can tell yourself everything is great. You can read the reports at the end of the month and announce 'we grew by 30%!' all the while hearing the rumbles from employees about how miserable they are.

You get to choose which story you listen to. Which reflection you see.

But just like that fresh cut and fancy outfit, it all fades away and the reflection you see the next morning isn't what it once was. Your hair is a mess again. Your pajamas aren't as pretty as that dress. Your teeth need brushed and your cool 5:00 shadow is now miffed.

So you start again. A new day. A new opportunity. A new reflection.

When you begin to listen to the story of what your employees are telling, it calls you to reflect on what is truly taking place. It causes you to ask questions internally about how you lead, about the culture you have designed, about the systems you have created, and about how you may or may not be empowering your team.

And there's a truth to each of these stories. But there is also hope that you have the power to change the reflection.

If you are constantly watching people quit- there's a reason.
If you are consistently struggling to find high performers- there's a reason.
If you are losing people to other organizations- there's a reason.

If you are frustrated and tired of the weariness of leadership- there's a reason.

And that reason lies within.

It's time to ask yourself the hard questions. More importantly, it's time to spend a moment with your reflection and respond to these hard questions with truth, vulnerability, and clarity.

How are you investing in your growth as a person?
Who have you surrounded yourself with professionally and personally?
Who are you learning from?
How are you implementing what you are learning and how is it helping you?
Have you found a place of contentment within?
Are you listening to the feedback others are sharing?
What are you noticing about others when you are around them?
What is your greatest struggle in life?
Why is this a struggle?
What is your dream, how long have you had this dream, and what does it mean to you?
Who are you sharing your thoughts and ideas with?
Why did you read this book?
What other books are you reading?
What do you want out of life?

Finally- What reflection do you want to see when you view the world around you?

When you take part in responding to these questions and consider the reflection you are living, it changes how you approach life. You become much more aware of your actions, words, and thoughts. You become more aware of how everything is connected. You become more engaged with yourself and with others.

We call this way of living mindfulness.

When you live from a place of mindfulness, you become healthier, more grateful and live from the deepest part of your humanity.

And that, my friend, is what being a great leader is about. Living from your deepest humanity and providing safe space for others to do the same.

When you do that- hiring and keeping great people will be the least of your worries.

Thank you for taking the time to invest in yourself, your team, and your culture. I know that as you put the principles you learned in 'How to Hire and Keep Great People' to work, they will result in a return that will be measurable far beyond money or profits.

Mitch is ready to empower the way you lead. When you're ready to design great culture, find great people, and build your dream team- just let us know.

Booking: mitch@mitchgraymedia.com
Web: www.mitchgraymedia.com

CPSIA information can be obtained
at www.ICGtesting.com
Printed in the USA
LVHW051112090123
736756LV00011B/1126

9 781667 186832